Migrant Earth

Other books by Ramón Mesa Ledesma

Children's
Tomás and the Magic Race Cars

Poetry/Prose
Migrant Sun

Migrant Earth

Ramón Mesa Ledesma

ISBN: 979-8-218-49286-1

Library of Congress Control Number: 2014933440

"Por nuestra cultura hablarán nuestros libros
(Our books shall speak for our culture)."
Quote courtesy of Floricanto Press.

First edition printed in 2014 by Floricanto Press
Second edition published in 2024 by Village Books Publishing
1200 11th Street
Bellingham, WA 98225

Book cover art by Jess Arashi Hara
2024 book design by Jill Flores
2024 edition proofread by Jill Twist

Printed in the USA by IngramSparks

This book is dedicated to the loved ones lost along the way—Marta, Rufina, Alvino, Maria, and Enrique—and those that remain—Chavelo, Manuel, Francisco, Raquel, Dolores, Juan, Linda, Mario, and Arturo. Your personal stories have inspired me to record our shared journey in hopes those who stand beside us and those that come after will understand their legacy and embrace the history we carved out of this fruitful land with our backs, strong will, and unrelenting spirit. My hope is these stories fill the void left by the silence of a journey often too painful to talk about. These stories are shared to build the cultural and historical foundation our loved ones can stand on long after the sun has set and we've made it safely home.

I pray we've earned your love and respect.

In the last days, God said, "I will pour out my Holy Spirit upon all mankind, and your sons and daughters shall prophesy, and your young men shall see visions, and your old men dream dreams."

— Acts 2:17, Living Bible

The Dream

And when my eyesight dimmed and my body was worn, arthritic and too bent to carry a hoe to the fields under the migrant sun, I lay down and dreamed we were free: three million and more brown migrant laborers in America, wanting little more than safe shelter, honest work, and the opportunity to raise our families upon the fertile soil that sustains us.

It's Just Temporary...

We were raised to believe, my siblings and I, that our early, humble circumstances were temporary. I have to laugh when I use the word humble. Humble, hell, we lived in dirty, rat-infested, dilapidated, migrant labor camps. Humble has an almost gallant, honorable, romantic ring to it, and I'm here to tell you there was nothing remotely romantic, gallant, or honorable about where and how we lived. I've seen flea-bitten stray dogs that lived better than we did. But this belief, that our circumstances were temporary, was my *padres'* incessant mantra. In our formative years, it seemed to seep into virtually every conversation we had about where we were and what we were doing.

I'm emphatic when I talk about this because as I look back, our very survival depended on this understanding at its most rudimentary level. After years of searching for this transformative idea, I have finally reached this understanding. And ultimately, the conundrum of how each of us survived, while four older siblings and countless friends didn't, has occupied more conversations over the years than I care to remember. All through adulthood, at birthday gatherings and holiday feasts, after a few beers or margaritas assuaged the emotional burden of survival, the conversation would invariable turn to the good old days, (a gross misnomer at best). Inevitably, at some point, someone asked the question that, after all these years, still occupied our thoughts and invaded the secret places of our dreams. "How did we make it out of those camps alive?"

And ultimately, the key to our survival was the message in our *padres'* mantra and the hope it engendered. At whatever disgraceful labor camp, in whatever state we found ourselves in, we were made to believe—to understand—we were merely visitors, not permanent residents. We were just passing through. Where we were was a necessary, but temporary, step to someplace better. Where we were was not the destination. And later, as adults, we probably subconsciously understood this while consciously, I'm sure we were looking for something more deeply spiritual, psychological, or philosophical to explain our survival. And the simplest of messages often have the most profound effects.

In the Beginning

Of my beginnings, I recall flashes: ancient images like cracked pictures in faded black and white on dusty shelves, abandoned to the quiet passing of time. I see scarred, brown faces, glimpses of unknown places, and mysterious spaces: a night street, illuminated by a defused, pale yellow light; an old abandoned pickup truck parked beside a filling station; a man's grease-stained face peering out a grimy window into a lonely, vacant night; an emaciated dog wandering an alley of forgotten, rusted car carcasses; and the odd image of a menacing butcher knife impaled above the inside of a door of a shack. Solitary images standing without narrative, life, or meaning. Without voices, they offer but brief windows into the time before my awakening, awareness, questioning, and understanding. They place me in silent moments among the echoing shadows of time. Seeking explanation, finding none, I watch them return in the vulnerable darkness of my sleep.

Eventually, a time arrived when life went from silent pictures to narrative forms. Like the flip of a light switch, I was suddenly aware of a different world outside my own. This juxtaposition of realities, one silent, one with words, was the catalyst to a narration that simultaneously became history and future.

It was a morning that began with a misting of light rain. It had given the strawberry field a fresh scent. The soil was rich in my nostrils as I worked alongside my family. The mid-morning sun was breaking through the dissolving, gray cloud cover, and it found us working a field without end. Suddenly aware of a prompting, a whisper maybe, possibly carried in the salty breeze off the ocean, I abruptly stood up and looked around for its origins. As I stood, I wondered why and how everything had inexplicably changed. The strawberry leaves and surrounding fir trees appeared a vibrant, more colorful green, the berries a richer red, and the sky, a blue I didn't recognize, had replaced the dull gray clouds. I looked at *Mamá* and my brothers and sisters for confirmation they were experiencing the same transformation, but they were busy picking, and none seemed affected.

Much later, I came to know that moment as one of my awakenings. Others would follow. This awakening gave way to a new awareness. Within this awareness began my questioning. Questioning that led to understanding. Not that I have ever understood the mysteries of life, why some people came and remained while others were lost, but an understanding that led to comfort. Not that I have ever been comfortable in the understanding I have attained. But I can say I feel I'm on the path, moving day by day toward understanding the ultimate knowledge of no final, earthly destination, but confident in the effort and sincerity of the journey. It's within this effort, within this journey, moving on this path toward a deeper awareness, knowledge, and understanding, that these stories find life.

Migrant Earth

With hoe, back, and sacrifice
We attempted to impose our will
Upon this migrant earth we lived with.
And as we aged,
The passing of the seasons
Rewarded strength and youth.

And it was plus one
Or minus one,
In life through the seasons:
A life without reason.

Some years when the balance
Of elements was benevolently aligned,
The harvest was full and rich.
But others…
When the frigid winds colluded
With the drenching rains,
The moon and stars
Turned against us.

And it was plus one
Or minus one,
In life through the seasons:
A life without reason.
Sometimes it felt like treason.

Sometimes we watered
With our tears.
Sometimes we fed it with our flesh.
Sometimes in fear
We cursed it,
But in the end, like parent and child,
Together we grew enmeshed.

And comes a time
When strong hands
Become weak and arthritic:
When our gait slows
And eyesight dims:
When all we've built
Turns to seed and weeds
And the children of our loins
Leave and don't return…

Then all that will remain,
All that we will have
Is the earth…
And the earth will
Welcome us,
Take us home
Into its cold embrace.
And it is there,
In our final rest
We'll find our
Eluded peace.

Migrant Earth.

Death Came Round

It was cold the night
The birds didn't sing.
It was cold the night
The bells didn't ring.

Everyone huddled around
A hot, coal-fed
Potbelly stove.
Middle of the cabin.
Middle of the snow storm.
Middle of Montana.

Papá, wake up!
Mamá, don't forget!
Stoke that stove
Or we'll regret.

It was the night
The river froze.
It was the night
Our sins disclosed
The weak and the tired,
Or so the story goes.

It was the night
When all were sleeping.
It was the night
When death came creeping.
Death watched her—sister,
Slowly—
Silently—
Roll away.

No one up to
Stoke the fire.
No one up to see
Her move away.
From the middle
Of the cabin
In the middle
Of the storm,
To lay alone.
Death came slowly.
First blood froze,
Still no one rose.
Flesh got hard,
Death came close.

Then fragile heart stopped,
When cold was around,
And death came down
Without a sound
In Forsyth town.

Death came round.

The Water That Flows

The water that flows is my blood.
It flows red,
Through creeks, streams, and river beds
That evaporate into laden, ashed clouds,
And too heavy for them to bear,
The water returns to the fields
In droplets big as thumbs.

Waters gather and flow,
Down the mountains, into the valley
Where Fisher Creek runs
Through the pasture
Behind my home,
Where salmon return from
The ocean to spawn.

Salmon swim in waters
That are my own.

The water that flows is my blood.

Morning Courtyard

Like a fog in the warming sun, the shadows of sleep began to dissipate as I lay quietly, listening to a rooster crowing somewhere on the farm or in the darkness of my dreams. In the tree outside the window, robins chirped; below, contented chickens clucked, scavenging for food in the dirt. The sounds of an awakening courtyard enveloped me, gently nudging me out of darkness into light. Teetering between two worlds, I floated from one to another and back again. As the sun began to fill our bedroom and warm my face, my dreams faded. Keeping my eyes closed, I let the soothing farmyard sounds comfort me.

But suddenly, I felt myself being tugged out of my cozy warm stupor into full wakefulness. I lay for a few moments, listening. Where were the sounds of my siblings as they dressed for work, or my *padres* as they began their morning routine? To my surprise, no one was stirring.

I hesitated. Mornings on the farm were imbued with an eerie, mystical quality that gave me pause. I never liked being the first one up, alone in the stillness. Instead, I cultivated the habit of hovering between sleep and wakefulness, waiting for my siblings to rise before me. They thought I was lazy. I struggled with that, but found it easier to bear than facing early mornings alone.

I've never been able to explain my fear of mornings. Back then, I knew trying to explain it to my parents or older siblings would only add fuel to the already embarrassing way I was viewed in the family. Being known as *el llorón* was one thing; having them know I was afraid of something mysterious in the mornings would be altogether another. In a family of strong Mexican males, this six-year-old boy found that idea, and the ribbing that would ensue from it, unbearable.

On this particular morning, although I felt the ever-present fear, there was something altogether different, too. Something outside me, compelling me, enticing me out of bed. Curious, I overcame my fears for the moment and quietly, reluctantly, slipped out of bed in my underwear and T-shirt. As I did, I felt a heavy, ominous presence inhabiting or holding the house in a stillness that to this day sends shivers up my spine. As I approached the bedroom door, I half expected to be greeted by the presence, whatever it was, or, I thought, hopefully, the morning's first activities: *Papá* sitting at the kitchen table reading the Mexican paper and *Mamá* making coffee and preparing breakfast.

No such luck. The house was still and silent. Everyone was still asleep; not even *Papá's* thunderous snoring could be heard. I stopped. It felt so unusual to be the only one up and awake. But I braved the silence and walked quietly through a house suspended in time, toward the back door. If I hadn't discovered the force inside the house, I thought, perhaps it would reveal itself in the courtyard. Whatever the presence was, I felt sure it was guiding me. With some trepidation, I slowly opened the back door, and, making sure I didn't make a sound, gently closed it behind me. The summer sun was up, but I felt the coolness of the previous evening at my bare feet. As I sat down on the porch steps, the morning light illuminated the golden haystack; a full, lush garden; two small barns and the sagebrush-covered rattlesnake hills in the distance. Although I'd heard farmyard sounds when I woke, the farm was now bathed in a silence so complete, I could feel my heart beating and hear the blood coursing through my veins.

I sat there for a long moment, listening, waiting. I wasn't sure how long it had been since all sound had ceased. I suddenly questioned whether the silence was happening in me or outside of me. How it was happening was a mystery.

Then I felt the presence manifested in force. The one that had urged me out of bed and through the house and out to the back porch. By now I was so enraptured by the mystery, I was beyond fear. Something drew my attention toward the south end of the farm. It rolled, uninhibited, over the foothills and began to build in intensity as it traveled down toward the farm. Although I couldn't see anything, still I felt it move in a pulsating, overlapping motion. Like ocean waves undulating toward the shore, whatever-it-was moved across the farm. With my heart's eye, I felt it sweep by me like a tsunami. An emotional crescendo cloaked in silence, it came crashing down and across the farm in front of me. As it passed, it swept into and through me. This omnipresent force flooded the deepest recesses of my soul, invading and claiming every molecule and atom it touched and washed.

I felt completely awake and alert. I saw nothing, yet felt everything. What my eyes couldn't see, or my ears hear, my soul perceived with the clarity of a bell ringing in that quiet hour before dawn. I experienced panic, fear, awe, passion, reverence and love, all mixed into one. Somewhere, a deep and remote part of me recognized this force as if programmed to do so from the beginning of time. Completely unknown to me, it was as familiar as my own heartbeat. As it consumed me, it filled me until my emotions were overflowing. Reverent tears began to run down my face.

At last, unable to sustain watchfulness, I reached behind me for the doorknob. I opened the door and slipped quietly back into the house. I stood for a moment, taking in a house still suspended in time. Surprised, I walked back to our bedroom and crawled into our safe bed, kept warm by two others. As I began to drift back to sleep, I sensed I would wake to face the most important journey of my life.

It wasn't long before I became aware of the morning's familiar scents and stirring: coffee brewing; the sounds of *Mamá* in the kitchen starting breakfast; *Papá* rustling last night's paper.

When I woke I knew, with a child's understanding, that I had changed. Not in personality or character, but in reference and purpose. Until that morning, I had lived a carefree existence without thought or meaning or purpose. My anchors were family, culture, and the small farm we lived on. Not that a six-year-old would have been able to articulate this, but they were nevertheless present and innately real and important. All were still meaningful, yet now I felt undefined and unmotivated by them. Now what gave me purpose was the journey I had subconsciously acknowledged and accepted. It was a journey of, and for, meaning. Not that I was to create this meaning and purpose. I was to uncover it, to discover it in the world that lived within me. The dimensions or parameters of the journey before me were unclear. What was clear was my waking would commence the search for a different life.

Only years later, as an adult, would I come to some semblance of understanding of that mysterious experience. I'd always acknowledged the existence of a supreme being, but I made it into adulthood without any identity as a believer in a specific deity. For me, it had never been an intellectual or emotional stretch to believe that something as wonderful and breathtaking as life—mankind, nature, and all that surrounded it—did not come into being by happenstance. That would be like saying a bottle of Chateau Margaux evolved over millions of years to find itself corked in a dark green bottle in my wine cellar with no help from anyone. But God? What did I—or anyone—know of God?

But there was this thing: this ancient childhood experience I carried with me like a mystical dream. Perhaps I even questioned whether it had really happened. Time does that to even our most vivid experiences. Even important experiences are subject to the fluidness of time and the elasticity of memory.

I was thirty years old and working to define the next phase of my life. I had accomplished much of what I had early on committed to do. I was college educated, had a good and meaningful job, and was respected by my peers. I felt good about what I had accomplished and confident in what was yet to come. I was not experiencing any significant trauma or going through any trials.

In fact, I was lying in bed reading when I heard a whisper. It was audible enough to make me question whether I was alone. I looked around my bedroom. No one.

"Answer your door. I'm waiting for you!" the voice said. Not accustomed to hearing voices, I said, "What?"

Then, to prove myself sane, I got up, slipped on my bathrobe, and went to see if anyone was at my door. I opened it. No one. Nothing but an empty staircase leading to a dark parking lot full of cars.

Confused, but nevertheless amused, I smiled to myself and went back to bed. As I turned off my reading light I said,

"Okay, now that was weird!" I vowed never to tell this story to anyone, lest they think I was a bit off.

But as I tried to get to sleep, I found I could not. As I lay there in the dark, something I still can't explain happened. The scales of unbelief fell from my heart's eyes and I learned that God had once revealed Himself to me while I was still a child. Now, He was returning: come to claim what long ago He said was His. It wasn't a shout or a bell ringing that awakened me. It was a quiet whisper that said, "No, not the door to your dwelling, but the door to your heart. It's me, Jesus Christ. You've always known about me and now it's time to believe in me and let me in."

With the clarity of a pristine mountain spring, I understood the message. I came to know Christ, not from something I'd read or a person I'd listened to. He introduced Himself to me in a very personal and intimate way when I was a child on a small farm, and then He returned to me when I was an adult, alone in my bedroom, late one night. There was no mistaking His voice. There was no mistaking the message. And there was no mistaking my journey's end.

The next morning, on my way to work, I opened my front door to find a flyer from a local church lying on the floor. Someone had written on it, "We rang your doorbell last night. Come see us sometime." It felt good knowing He'd covered all contingencies.

Today, my journey for understanding the mysteries of God continues anew every morning as I rise and each evening as I retire.

Across the Valley

We were slender, bony bodies,
Baked golden brown,
Running through the summer sun.
There were endless stretches
Where time was suspended
And neither came nor went.
Nothing aged, and paradise
Waited to be born anew
Under the morning sun,
And dreams swam like
Fish in the ocean and
The milky light of the moon.

Rich, fertile brown dirt:
The foundation of life
Mingled with irrigation water,
Enriched with our blood and sweat.
And the corn grew ten feet tall,
Sugar beets, big and white
And the alfalfa, a deep, rich green.

ACROSS THE VALLEY

Cool, clear waters
Flowed in the shallow ditches
Above the fields
And traveled across the valley
From Ellensburg to Walla Walla:
From one farm to another,
Turning a sagebrush desert
Into orchards, vineyards,
And beautiful gardens.

Golden haystacks
Reached the blue sky.
Tower-like,
They peaked into the clouds,
And the pastures were lush,
And fences straight.
In balmy, warm summer nights,
The dogs curled up in the barn
While coyotes yipped.
Papá snored like
A rumbling freight train,
And we slept like newborn babies
Dreaming of Chinese kites
And Range Rider six guns.

Across the valley.

Watermelon Summer Evening

In what seemed an endless garden
To this child,
Papá grew the
Biggest, dark green skinned
Watermelons my brown eyes
Could encompass,
And my childhood arms
Could not carry.

In the August heat
They ripened
And in the cool of the
Late summer evening,
When we had worn out the sun
And it went hiding
Behind the Rattlesnake Hills,
We harvested them,
A wheelbarrow at a time.

WATERMELON SUMMER EVENING

WATERMELON SUMMER EVENING

Together, Juan, and Enrique
Maneuvered the wheelbarrow
Down to the garden where
Papá picked the ripest ones.
Filling the wheelbarrow full,
Papá helped them push,
And sometimes pull,
The heavily-burdened wheelbarrow,
Gently guiding it
Back to the courtyard
Where *Mamá* waited.

Papá picked one,
Put it in the tub
On the picnic table,
And *Mamá* sliced it
Long ways,
From end to end.
And into small hands,
Each were gifted
With a slice
Of lush, watery, red fruit,
Speckled black with seeds.
We carried our slices

WATERMELON SUMMER EVENING

Into the warm summer evening
And ate until there was nothing but rind.
And mischievous as we were,
We snapped the rind
Into small pieces and used
Them as weapons against
Anything that moved: black beetles
Flying moths, aggressive roosters
And sometimes each other,
(When *Mamá* or *Papá*
Weren't looking, of course).

When we finished our slice
We went back for another,
And another,
And another,
Until our bellies extended
Unnaturally and there
Was not one millimeter
Of room left to fill.
Our faces, hands, arms,

Chests, and bellies
Were a mess of sticky, red juice,
And then flies and mosquitoes were upon us.
And we played
Until bedtime when
Mamá lined us up
And hosed us off,
Then dried us clean
And marched us off to bed
Where we dreamed
The watermelon summer night away.

Watermelon summer evening.

Mamá Was a Dreamer

The thunder clapped across a malevolent sky.
The clouds opened up and the rains fell
On planted fields of sugar beets.
The heavy raindrops spattered the brown dirt
And filled my nose with the fresh,
Aromatic sent of irrigated loam.

Papá came in from walking the fields
To the shed where we waited to hear the news.

"The fields are wet and muddy," he explained.

It was then he released us
Upon the unsuspecting world of dimly
Lit barns, filled with freshly baled hay,
jack rabbit– and coyote-filled foothills, and acres of
Unexplored fields:
Our private playground.

We carefully put our hoes in the shed,
Lined them neatly against the wall,
Sharp and ready for tomorrow's
Weeds in drier fields.

MAMÁ WAS A DREAMER

My brothers took to the barns,
My sisters to the housework,
And I, to my favorite spot in the living room,
In front of the small picture window.
The window looked out over a lazy, winding driveway,
Meandering down to the forbidden railroad tracks
That lumbered with heavily burdened cars,
Carrying sleeping, grizzled, dirty old men.

Mamá's manual sewing machine sat there,
Before the portal of my imagination.
It was there she taught me to sew,
And there, she and I sewed away the rainy hours.
She taught me to darn the family socks
While she patched our clothes
And stitched the holes
Made by sharp knees and growing elbows.

It was there I was initiated
Into her magical world of dreams…
Set to the music
Of the whirring sewing machine.
As she pumped her feet,
The melodic, metronome cadence of the
Cast-iron black wheel
accompanied her hypnotic voice.
While she sewed, she dreamed,
And while she dreamed, I sat, mesmerized,
Transfixed by her soft Spanish voice.
Heard above the song of the big black wheel.

And she would say:

If you can dream them, *M'ijo*,
You can touch them,
And if you can touch them,
They will give you hope,
And hope is yours to keep—for all eternity.

She talked about her children,
And I learned about myself.
And she said I was a kind boy,
Sensitive and caring.
That someday, I would become a *consejero*.

I didn't know what a *consejero* was,
But I knew it had to be someone good.
That I was someone good.

Like a mysterious *bruja*
Foretelling my future,
I felt her eyes
Peer into my soul
And pierce the folds of time,
Ancient and young,
Waiting to be born within me.

MAMÁ WAS A DREAMER

As she sewed and talked,
Her words mixed with
The scent of boiling *canela*.
Together they swirled around her,
Filling the room and my senses,
And through the magic of her voice
With the backdrop of
The melodic sound of the
Cast-iron black wheel,
Flowed the rivers of my dreams.

And *Mamá* knew...
She had to teach me to dream,
That dreams gave life to hope,
And within this hope,
My future would be discovered.

The rain specked the window.
The sewing machine whirred,
And *Mamá* dreamed.
I listened to her voice,
Conjuring dreams that vowed to
Transcend the weight of our poverty.

MAMÁ WAS A DREAMER

Along the periphery of my imagination,
I could hear the cadence of the train in the distance,
Clang-clang, clang-clang, clang-clang,
Carrying me in new clothes to exotic,
Faraway places.

Those were lean times.
Mamá patched our clothes to last
Through lean times.
Mamá bound our spirits to survive
Through all times.

And she would say:

If you can dream them, *M'ijo*,
You can touch them,
And if you can touch them,
They will give you hope,
And hope is yours to keep—for all eternity.

God created rainy days
And man built picture windows
And whirring sewing machines
For dreamers.

Mamá was a dreamer,
And I...
I am the dreamer's son.

The thunder clapped across a malevolent sky.

Driveways and Hallways

By the early 1950s my *padres* had saved enough money to stop our migrant wanderings and buy a thirty-acre farm in rural Outlook, Washington. To us, it was like reaching the proverbial Promised Land. Not that God had led my *padres* out of Mexico and promised them sanctuary—but hard work, diligence, and sacrifice, ultimately, had their own reward. It had been too late for four of my older siblings who died in childhood along the way. Their untimely deaths and our safety had to have weighed heavily on my *padres'* minds when they bought the farm. For the moment, the future appeared safe within the confines of a piece of land we could call our own. This was when the word "home" first entered our family's lexicon. It had been a long time coming. Neither of my *padres* had seen home, as in permanent ownership, ever.

Within this magical window of opportunity, I approached my first day of school.

Most American children's first day of school is simply an extension of informal acculturation, formalized in the classroom setting. Within the Anglo family, for the most part, a child is nurtured: expected and encouraged to have no other responsibility aside from being a child and engaging in fun, and sometimes frivolous, activities. For them, beginning school is a continuation of that expectation, albeit with added intellectual rigor and social training to encourage conformity. It's a step up, not a leap.

My introduction to formalized education was a giant leap, thanks to the complex reality of being born into a large Mexican migrant-worker family. I didn't know at the time, but would soon learn, that the Anglo children didn't meet the rising sun in the fields, nor did its setting find them returning home with aching backs and hoes balanced on their tired shoulders. Acquiring that knowledge would be the inception of future cognitive dissonance for me.

That morning, I woke from a long night of fitful sleep, troubled by a dream of being lost and chased by a snarling wolf. My breath came quick and shallow; the dream had ended in an emotional montage of fear and anxiety and left me shaken. I vaguely realized, when I slipped quietly from beneath the cotton blanket and placed my small feet on the worn linoleum floor, that life as I'd known it would soon be a distant memory. My child's mind really was not quite ready for the mysteries of a formalized education in Anglo society—nor for my introduction to the brutal fieldwork that accompanied starting school in my family.

My anxiety lay between the darkness of my dreams and the reality the morning light would illuminate; between what I thought I knew and the as yet unknown truth; between the dual demands of carrying your load in the fields and being successful in Anglo school. Although I'd never been to school, I understood its significance by observing my *padres'* serious faces and listening to their reverent tones whenever they talked about it with my siblings. My older siblings understood, as I would eventually: future success was not to be found in the migrant fields, but it rode on our efforts there. If we were ever going to leave the fields— and that was our *padres'* expectation—we had to be successful in the classroom and work hard in the fields. The immediate fruits of hard labor were essential: what profit we won from the lush fields of sugar beets, asparagus, and alfalfa paid our taxes and supported us through our years in school. Our future germinated in the fields and was harvested in the classroom.

But to us children, the dual burden was all we felt: the summer heat on our necks and backs and the winter cold that froze our fingers and toes. Ultimately, we came to the understanding that one was not achieved without the other. Until then, we resented the hard work and sometimes even our *padres*.

So I was filled with a myriad of emotions that fateful morning—the least of which were nocturnal images of being lost or ravaged by a wolf. That the dreams might be symbolic of what I was about to face was not clear, but also not completely lost on me.

I was entering a culture I didn't quite understand. Since Spanish was our primary language, we never spoke English with our *padres*. That would have been seen as disrespectful to them and dismissive of our proud culture. It would have been abandoning the difference we knew defined us and made us special.

Yet, I felt sick at the idea of being thought dumb or slow because I couldn't explain myself or understand what was expected of me. Yes, eight siblings had gone to school before me, but it wasn't as if they'd come home each day ready to teach me everything they'd learned. At home, I didn't see anyone working math problems, or reading Jules Verne or Jane Austen. With all the work to be done in the fields, at home, no one had time for academic pursuits. And although academics were strongly encouraged, if not demanded, the two pursuits had their well-established places: one took place at school and the other at home. As I look back at my school days, I can't remember having even one conversation with my *padres* about homework, papers, books, or even grades. I do, on the other hand, recall the heavy burden of the unspoken expectation that we would work hard—and succeed.

On that memorable day, I knew only that school and work in the fields were both in my immediate future. Before we were school-age, my siblings and I had no defined work duties. Now, for me, that period of relative freedom would come to an abrupt end. Old enough to start school, I was also old enough to sharpen and work the business end of a long-handled hoe: backbreaking, mind-numbing work in the field under a blazing, unrelenting sun. That was the beginning of *Papá*'s harsh, no-nonsense apprenticeship into field labor and expectations of long, disciplined days of hard work, and the end of daydreams about Radio Flyers, Schwinn bicycles, and languid summer days.

Leading up to my first day of school, when pressed, *Mamá* had talked of *muchos dias, semanas, y meses*, and said not to bother her with it anymore. But I had minimal understanding of time and could not grasp the increments she offered. I knew only of the sun rising in the mornings and mysteriously disappearing in the evening. The last thing I remember before waking up in the morning was moonlight spilling through the window and the spidery shadows of the willow branches dancing on the walls beside our bed.

Like my older brothers and sisters before me, I had waited and endured, but perhaps less patiently than they. To say I was a high-strung, anxious child would be an understatement. *Mamá*, a patient angel, had many school-related conversations with me, and they always ended the same. Sitting at my bedside, tired of explaining, on numerous occasions, she pulled the covers over my head, gently shoved my head onto my pillow, and told me to go to sleep. When I woke, I would be one day closer to my first day of school. And furthermore, if I didn't close my eyes and go to sleep, time would not move forward, but backward and when I woke, I would be younger and further from the big day. I could hear her smile as she turned the light off.

Now, the morning was finally here. The intense heat of summer had dissipated from the evenings and early mornings. This morning, the sun was bright, if a bit defused, as it splashed through the window to the warm floor beneath my feet. I paused to imagine the long walk down the potholed gravel driveway that would lead me to things unknown. Looking out the window near the bed I shared with two brothers, one older and one younger, I saw only a few clouds in the sky. I took a deliberate breath, taking in the last fleeting images of my last carefree childhood summer. I heard my older brothers and sisters coming in from the fields and knew I needed to hurry. Mario, a few years younger, was still asleep, rolled in a ball, oblivious to anything beyond his carefree dreams and warmth of his sleep cocoon.

My brothers and sisters cleaned up for school while I dressed with feverish excitement. As I hurriedly consumed my Cream of Wheat and toast, not wanting to be late, *Mamá* watched and smiled. Although the novelty of another child starting school was lost on her long ago, she tolerated my excitement. As long as I didn't squeal, scream, or run around like a chicken whose head she'd just whacked off for tonight's dinner, she allowed me my joy.

Mamá was not an effusive person. The light in your eyes could explode like Chinese fireworks and your skin could tingle with goose bumps, but you were not allowed to run, yipping and yelping, chasing your tail like a golden retriever. *Mamá* had experienced too much heartbreak to allow herself or her loved ones too much joy. She loved *Dios*, but I don't think she trusted Him, especially with her precious jewels: her lovely brown children.

But of course the fact that *Mamá* had been there eight times before didn't in any way diminish my excitement. (Though knowing there were three behind me probably diminished hers!) The prospect of joining the elite eight I loved, and even worshiped a bit, only heightened my anticipation. How desperately I had longed to grow up and follow them, with only the slightest understanding of the sometimes harsh and complicated nature of the destination!

I was the first out the door. Raquel, Dolores, Juan, Enrique, and finally Francisco, followed. We walked the driveway to the bus stop, over and beyond the railroad tracks—past the limits of my imagination. I could not conjure up what awaited me or guess how ill-prepared I was to enter this mysterious world, filled with things my siblings warned me about, but were beyond my understanding. I had so little experience outside my Mexican family moorings, how could they explain?

As we walked, I indulged in wild speculation, trying to fill the void between what I had gleaned and what I naively wanted to believe. Was school like the farm on a summer's day with haystacks, fences, barns, and miles of open sky and dirt play fields? Were there crystal streams of invigorating cool water coming out of the hills, running through the playgrounds? Did we get to swim and play in them when we wanted? Were the kids like my brothers and sisters, who loved to play away the warm summer days? Where the kids Mexican or white, or some of each? Were my teachers going to be like my parents: a patient, loving, compassionate mother and a strong, stern father? Was the food like *Mamá*'s: spicy and delicious? Did we get to take naps in the afternoon and wake to the scents of boiling *canela* on the stove, wafting through the schoolhouse? The questions swarmed in an ocean of excitement and trepidation.

I had never been anywhere without my *padres* or a small cadre of older siblings to accompany me. I was afraid I might not be as tough as the rest. Actually, I knew I wasn't. And I knew little of this other culture. What I did know was gleaned from stolen glances, fragments of conversations. On the awkward occasion we were around Anglos, their unfamiliar words seemed sharply hurled from scornful faces. They seemed harsh and looked and sounded ugly, simply by vocal inflection and distorted faces.

Whether my *padres* had purposely taught me to fear Anglos to protect me, or I intuitively picked up this fear from their conversations, I've never been able to say. "They're not like us. They neglect their children and throw away old people like we throw out scraps for the pigs." I'd heard it a hundred times. What I heard was fear, and what I saw, I didn't trust. The little experience I'd had around the Anglos had taught me how different we were from them. And it went much deeper than their sallow, colorless skin. In my family and culture, our brown skin was a source of great pride. It was only after being in school a short while, I began to hear the Anglo kids talking disparagingly about our color. I didn't understand this, and when I related their comments to *Papá*, he laughed. He said, "They're jealous." He once showed me pictures in a magazine called *Look*, of

Anglos sunbathing. "They want to be brown like us," he said, and shook his head.

Despite my doubts, I was excited: since my older siblings were making it, I was hopeful I could too. And so I willingly headed into the unknown, my *Mamá*'s reassurance ringing in my ears: "If you get scared, remember, your brothers and sisters will be all around you." I innately understood that Mexican families stuck together and looked after their own and felt safer.

After a short distance, I looked back once, maybe to gain perspective, or to ground myself in the knowledge that although everything before me was changing, behind me everything I knew was not. And that's when I saw her, standing in the kitchen doorway, wiping her hands on her apron, watching us playfully walking away from her. Linda and Mario were seated at her feet, curious. Arturo played nearby. I recall wondering what was going through *Mamá*'s mind. Throughout my childhood, I encountered this same undecipherable, inscrutable image: *Mamá* watching us with a wistful air, her brow furrowed. She gazed into her apron and nervously dried her hands of soapy dish water. The look seemed worried, if not a bit prayerful, in its watchfulness. Sifting these images in my adult mind, I'm reminded of similar memories throughout the years. One was of *Mamá* sitting on a bench seat with my younger brothers, Mario and Arturo, and my sister, Linda, outside the Greyhound bus depot in Goldendale, Washington, watching me get on a bus that would take me to the induction center in Yakima. I had been drafted into the military during the Vietnam War. Four older brothers had gone before me. Again, watching her children leave was nothing new. As the bus sped off, I turned to look one last time, maybe for the same reason I did as a child: to gain perspective, or ground myself in the knowledge that nothing behind me was changing, in hopes that it would help me with the growing fear in my gut and gnawing sense of doom darkening my thoughts as I headed off to war. I have always found it easier to leave for unknowns with the knowledge I was grounded in a known to which I belonged. That which I claimed ownership of, and which claimed ownership of me. Regardless of what I faced ahead, the fact I was rooted to a familiar soil and belonged to a family that loved and worried about me made all the difference.

Then too, I wondered what she was thinking. It was not until many years later that I glimpsed what might have been going through her mind, as I stood at an airport window watching one of my daughters leave me, on her way to college thousands of miles away. Like my mother before me, I had no idea what fate would befall this vulnerable young one I so deeply loved. I stood powerless before a universe I didn't trust or understand and had to rely on my prayers and faith to sustain me and, hopefully, protect her. As tears streamed down my checks, blurring the airplane image as it taxied away, I finally understood what *Mamá* must have felt each time one of us walked away from her. At that moment, I was thankful I would not be doing it more than a couple times. I knew I did not have her emotional strength to survive more than a few of these leavings.

After turning from *Mamá*'s face and focusing on my journey beyond the railroad tracks, I recall audibly whispering to myself that I could turn back at any time. If I got down to the mailboxes and didn't want to go to school, I didn't have to. I could turn around and return home to the safety of the front steps beside Linda, Mario, and Arturo. But I also knew it wasn't so. I knew when I had crossed the railroad tracks, I'd already passed the point of no return. And anyway, in my family, turning back, retreating, or giving up had never been an option. (Especially in the fields, when you committed to a row, you finished it, come hot sun, snow, or driving rain.) *Papá* taught us when you committed to something, you rode it out. Not that I was always able to ride it out to his or my own satisfaction, in childhood or adulthood. Much later, I was to learn that giving up or quitting was not only the option of the weak, but sometimes of the wise as well. At one time or another, I have been both.

I looked to the west, and in the distance a big yellow school bus was rounding a corner and coming into view. Following close behind was a long, gray funnel of dust that eventually disappeared into the warm morning air. I quickly took hold of Raquel's hand. As the now-gigantic bus slowed, I hid behind her. She laughed, and when it stopped she attempted unsuccessfully to push me up the steps ahead of her. When I wouldn't go, she pulled me up behind her.

When we got to the last step, she claimed the front bench seat on the right and sat me on the inside, next to the window, then scooted in beside me. I think she was trying to make sure I felt safe. Or, maybe she was afraid I would bolt for the door and run before the bus driver closed it. She held my hand and smiled reassuringly as the rest of my siblings marched on and took seats all around us.

As the door closed and the bus slowly pulled away, I looked at her, and her smile had the desired effect. Feeling momentarily comforted, I turned my gaze back to our small farm and watched it slowly fade in the distance as we passed white barns and farm houses with grazing cattle in pastures surrounded by barbed wire fences. Although this world was not a new one, everything was somehow new when viewed for the first time from the vantage point of a big yellow school bus lumbering along the gravel country road with billowing dust that obscured, and as far as I could tell, erased everything behind it. My world was evolving before my eyes and soon I would be too. I sat quietly mesmerized, unable to take my eyes from the widow, watching the metamorphosis take place before me and feeling it begin to change me.

I looked at Raquel as she sat, straight, back braced against the firm, forest green bench seat. Her chin was soft but strong, and her eyes sparked confidently. She was facing forward with her shoulders squared, looking to meet the future with the confidence of someone who was neither afraid nor intimidated by it. I intuitively understood I was to do the same. Imitating her, I turned and squared my fragile shoulders and focused forward as well. I took a deep breath and smiled to myself. And there was something about facing forward, with chin up and shoulders back, that reassured and helped create a bit of needed confidence. The solid posture helped me move through and past my dissolving past to face the advancing future. I knew I had little time, but somehow understood some preparation was necessary to gain some semblance of inner stability.

Little did I know, I would use the same calming deep-breathing technique repeatedly to face future challenges: flying in Vietnam, going to college, getting married, having children, and going through a divorce. As I look back on that moment, I'm struck by the realization of how a decision made in an instant by one so innocent and young could so strongly define a destiny. I looked at Raquel as she sat beside me. She smoothed out her ironed cotton dress, set her face to the oncoming future, and just faced it. No crying, moaning, or complaining—just faced it. Could I do less?

Daunting as the first step was, it was done. The bus raced past ripening corn and sugar beet fields, leaving all I knew behind. I knew this to be a time when childhood was a harvest moon, shining like a Halloween pumpkin, illuminating a passionate, kind people, sleeping on a mystic farm, nestled somewhere in the warmth of an ancient dream.

Excitement dissipated and fear turned to terror as the bus stopped in front of the redbrick school building. We disembarked to swim in a sea of children of varying ages and sizes, undulating in waves, toward the front doors of the building. Everyone, from the oldest to the youngest, were talking, laughing, or yelling, for it was the first day of school and no one seemed able to contain their excitement. I grabbed Raquel's hand with both of my tiny hands and hung on; letting go would certainly mean being lost in the waves of children, moving me out to sea to be lost forever. Altogether, my family group swarmed slowly and intentionally toward the front doors, where everything slowed. There, the mob converged into two lines to get in the building through narrow doorways.

Raquel, as you might have guessed by now, was my designated guide. She was a veteran in the fourth grade and knew all about school. As I looked up at her, I could tell she wasn't the least bit intimidated, and I took no small amount of comfort in that. Raquel, I recall, was rarely afraid or befuddled of anything. She was self-assured, confident, perky, and read a lot, which I was sure made her very smart. Most of all, I looked up to her because she would never allow herself to be bossed by my older brothers. She was the logical choice to help me on my first day of school.

Hand in hand, we walked up the stairs and through the front doors, into the main hall that led us past the principal's office on the left. Just past the office, we came to a huge room where many dark-stained wooden chairs sat fixed and facing one direction. The chairs were of a kind I had never seen before. I asked her how they worked, and she stopped for a minute and pulled me aside to show me. The chair sat fixed to the concrete floor and the bottom folded up neatly into the top part. She pulled the bottom part down and sat in it, demonstrating. I was amazed.

The floor was smooth beige concrete, and it slanted forward so that if I dropped one of my marbles, it would roll swiftly down and clank loudly at the base of a raised stage at the very end of the room. Raquel called the massive room an auditorium, whatever that was. She said it was where meetings and performances were held. She told me I would learn all about it later, but for now, not to think too much about it because we had to find my classroom, wherever and whatever that was. I let it go and continued to follow alongside her.

"Ramón," she said, as we walked. "You're hurting my hand. Don't squeeze so hard." I smiled, but didn't loosen my grip. There were kids everywhere, and I could still get lost.

I watched as older brothers and sisters, one by one, disappeared into closed spaces she once again called classrooms. As we walked around corners and down corridors, everything echoed loudly of high-pitched voices and thundering feet, until I was in a state of internal frenzy. The farther we walked, more kids disappeared into mysterious, secret rooms hidden behind wire-reinforced thickly windowed doors. I began to worry because slowly, everyone was disappearing. My sister Dolores was the first to disappear, followed by Juan, and last, Enrique. I never knew what happened to Francisco.

I don't recall when it happened, but I became acutely aware of walking with Raquel down a very long hallway. Doors were closing, one after another, and then it became relatively quiet but for the sounds of the two of us rustling along and the percussive sound of Raquel's hard-soled shoes, reverberating sharply off the walls behind us. I momentarily strained to look behind me for the origins of the sharp sounds. Raquel just smiled and pulled me along.

As classrooms filled, doors along the corridor closed, and I could see soundless lips, speaking in a foreign tongue. At the front of most rooms stood wrinkled, pallid-skinned women with graying hair tied aloft in tight buns. These women gestured mechanically, peering with dispassionate and stern eyes. What I sensed made me instantly cautious and afraid of them. To this day, I don't know how or why, but at that moment, I was afraid of them. I somehow feared their potential to extinguish my aboriginal intuitiveness and poorly channel my imaginative inquisitiveness. I felt physically queasy and strangely, spiritually uneasy. I understand the fear better today, but it's from a vantage point of maturing years and a lot of experience. It was the intuition that the old ways had to be extinguished for the civilizing Anglo educational inculcating process to be effective. I sensed the danger, even though I didn't know about it at the time.

It has been used by our government with the Native American children and by the Catholic Church in Latin America to disastrous cultural effects.

I readjusted my ever-tightening grip on Raquel's soft hand while looking up at her once again for reassurance. As long as I was moored to her hand, I determined I was still relatively safe. As we neared the end of this long hallway, Raquel stopped and turned to face the last open door on the left. She looked up at the room number and softly murmured to herself that this was my room. She then looked at the name on the door and looked into the room, and everything apparently matched because she smiled down at me. "Yup, this is your room, Ramón, and that lady at the front of the class is your teacher."

Raquel stepped confidently into the classroom, but I held my ground outside the doorway, unsure I wanted to enter. I pulled her back across the threshold and down to my level. I put my cheek on hers and whispered so no one else could hear.

"Where are all the Mexican kids?" I asked in Spanish.

"There aren't very many of us here," she whispered.

"Does the teacher speak Spanish?"

"I don't think so, but remember, we aren't allowed to speak Spanish here. From now on I don't want you to speak Spanish to anyone. This is the time to practice your English."

"How am I going to understand her if she doesn't speak Spanish?"

"Ramón, you can speak and understand a little English. School is the place where you're going to learn to speak it better. Don't worry so much. Your brothers and sisters all started here, and remember we're going to be all around you," she said as she gently tugged me into the room. I wasn't the least bit convinced I was going to be okay, but at the moment, I didn't have much choice. It wasn't as if I hadn't already crossed the railroad tracks.

Her words returned to me in echoes, "Your brothers and sisters all started here." The expectation for me to be successful here as well was clear. In spite of feeling light-headed, I acquiesced, and reluctantly followed along.

"Your teacher's name is Miss Starr," Raquel said. As the teacher approached, I noticed she wasn't wrinkly like the others I'd seen, and her hair was not bundled up on top of her head. Her skin was smooth, and she had long, beautiful, flowing auburn hair that hung gracefully about her shoulders. She smiled as she knelt before me, and her eyes spoke reassuringly. Visions and fears of wrinkled, pallid-skinned women with graying hair disappeared. She had beautiful white teeth, and her breath had a Juicy Fruit scent.

I didn't feel as bad when Raquel gave her my hand and she led me to one of the three remaining chairs in the last row. I sat, turned, and saw Raquel calmly standing at the threshold of the door, watching me. I motioned for her to sit next to me and struggled to comprehend why she wouldn't. The last thing I recall seeing before my vision blurred with tears that quickly became a stream down my cheeks and neck, disappearing under my hand-me-down white shirt, was Raquel, backing out of the room, waving goodbye, and vanishing. I wanted to get up and follow her. I was afraid to, and afraid not to, so I sat immobilized, looking at the place I'd last seen her. Despite the tears that blurred my vision, to this present day, as an old man, the empty doorway is clearly, indelibly, etched in my mind's eye.

Sweet-Corn Courtyard

Papá waited until the sun went down
And the cool western breeze
Carried the day's heat away
Before he built a fire
In the middle of the courtyard.
On it, he placed a metal tub
Full of salty water.
And as we waited for the water to boil,
Mamá set us in front
Of the wheelbarrow, full of
Freshly picked corn
From the garden.

Our job was to remove the
Leafy husk and golden
Tassels to expose
The ripe, yellow corn.
We stood around
Shirtless, shoeless,
In the waning light,
Warmed by fire.

When the water boiled.
Mamá and *Papá*
Carefully placed naked,
Golden corn into the
The water, while we skipped
And played…waiting.

SWEET-CORN COURTYARD

Minutes later, *Mamá*
Filled a waiting platter
With steaming hot corn
On the cob…
When they cooled sufficiently,
We grabbed the cobs
With our tiny hands
And twirled them
On sticks of sweet butter
Until the cobs were dripping
With butter.
Mamá salted them and
We ate until our
Stomachs were full
And faces and bare chests
Dripped, buttery and salty.

Sweet-corn courtyard.

I Watched You

For Mr. Montgomery

From behind shy, brown, curious eyes,
I watched you make your way around the room.
It was a spring afternoon,
The kind that gives a brown boy hope
That life won't always be
A cold, dark winter of frozen fields,
Hand-me-downs,
Dirty hands and elbows,
And unrequited prayers.

You were walking up the row,
Talking to Robert Allen and
Listening to María Gamboa's question:
Making comments and corrections.
You were picking up homework
And making notations
In your frayed, black grade book.

You smiled at Ramona Marquez,
And laughed with Carlos Cruz.
And when you got to me,
Amid all the activity,
You stopped and laid your
Soap-scented hand on my right shoulder.

I WATCHED YOU

You kneeled on one knee,
And met me eye to eye.
I remember a kind smile
Behind benevolent eyes.

On occasion the soap scent
Mysteriously returns.
It's a brand I don't recall,
But my nose remembers it all.

I've encountered the scent
A few times over the years,
And always—
The memory of your smile is invariably attached to it.

It's been fifty years
And even though I don't recall what you said to me,
A Mexican boy
Of no particular importance
In your life, or anyone else's.
I remember the kindness
In your eyes, and the feel of your strong hand.
Kindness is like that.
It stays in the flesh—and heart:
The places one is touched.

I WATCHED YOU

I have a special place I store
That memory.
And when life gets out of focus,
And I don't feel worthy,
I remember the smile,
The touch,
And the scent,
And they remind me
Of how one person
Thought I was,
And I smile.

I watched you.

Shopping with *Mamá*

For the most part, I find shopping to be a pleasant enough experience. But when we were children, for *Mamá*, shopping was an enterprise fraught with a multitude of complications that started, but certainly did not end, with the fact that she could not speak, read, or write in English. She was equally unable to read or write in her native tongue of Spanish. My grandfather was obviously not into education. I don't think *Mamá* or any of her siblings ever attended any kind of schooling.

And then there was that numbers thing. She didn't understand the American money system. Throw in being part of a large, poor family of migrant laborers with one foot in the Mexican culture and the other in the United States of America, and you have what we were up against.

Our cultural differences were most evident when we left the labor camp every few weeks to shop for our necessities. The clash was usually ameliorated by the cool presence of my two older sisters, Raquel and Dolores. They spoke English better than the rest of us and were smart, non-confrontational, pretty, and patient: none of which we boys would ever be accused of!

When *Mamá* went shopping, some of us (meaning her sons) tagged along, not because we wanted to help, but because we wanted to run the streets like feral puppies, exploring a new world of concrete sidewalks, storefront windows, movie theaters, and an infinite variety of colorful new clothes. Going to town held an endless fascination for us.

And to be truthful, we were usually little more than a nuisance to *Mamá*, and probably an impediment to her goal: the seamless, problem-free, acquisition of goods. I, acutely conscious of how we stood out among the Anglos and desperately wanting not to be seen in the glare of those differences, shied away from being of any use at all. When we hit town, I was often the first to walk away from *Mamá*. At other times, I would simply slink along in the shadow of the Mexican lady and her throng of brown children, hoping I would not be called upon to help. On occasion, when she looked for me, I abandoned her like Saint Peter denying Jesus. Sometimes, I escaped without notice. Other times, she caught me and let me know with a scowl and a few choice words that I was not the honorable son she expected me to be. That invariably led to a flood of tears, on my part, not hers.

When she hit the grocery store, *Mamá* would confidently grab a cart, and up one aisle and down the other she'd go. Since she couldn't read, she depended on pictures and familiar logos to find what she needed: baking powder, salt, sugar, lard, bread, pinto beans, and flour were among the staples that had readily recognizable logos.

Her dependence on pictures and logos might have caused some observers to question her intelligence. But if you ever had to deal with her, you knew better. Regardless of her deficits, her strong personality, intuitive nature, determination to succeed, and no-nonsense attitude made her worthy of respect and admiration.

On one particular occasion, when I was unable to escape grocery duty, I personally witnessed a grocery shopping excursion that had all the makings for disaster. We were in a grocery store on the north side of Mount Vernon, Washington, with four carts filled to overflowing with foodstuffs of all kinds. *Mamá* had the lead cart, followed by Dolores, then Raquel, and then me, commandeering the last. The checker probably gave it little thought when *Mamá* emerged from the aisle with a full cart. When Dolores followed directly behind her, also with a full cart, she must have felt like it was the store's lucky day. But when Raquel appeared with the third cart, just as full, she must have begun to worry. I remember how her eyes grew wide when she saw me struggling to control the last one. She craned her long, skinny neck to determine if more were forthcoming. Considering the work she was about to undertake, perhaps she was thinking she should've taken the day off. Too late.

Without hesitation, *Mamá* began to unload her cart. As she did so, she nodded, letting Raquel and Dolores know she wanted them to take their places beside her, helping her empty the carts. As I recall, of all of us, Raquel and Dolores were the best with numbers. They were always out front on any occasion that required handling money. *Mamá* confidently deferred to them when the farmer paid our wages at the end of the week. Depending on the farm we were working on, sometimes a farmer paid with a check, and at others, in cash. The checks were always made out to *Mamá*. When it was time to cash them, Raquel or Dolores helped her scrawl her fairly legible name, *Rosa Ledesma*, on the back. Her signature comprised the only two words *Mamá* recognized and could write.

But together, *Mamá*, Raquel, and Dolores were able to decipher all the intricacies of the modern grocery store. Why she ever wanted me along was perplexing. When it came to money, I was not the person she needed. What I knew about money could be summed up in a fifteen-cent ice cream sundae. Perhaps *Mamá* simple did not understand I wasn't as bright as I appeared—or acted.

On this occasion, I was bright enough to see that the checker was worried—I thought, perhaps it was just the prospect of accurately ringing up four cartloads of groceries in succession that had her concerned. But, drawing a deep breath, she stated to manually ring up each item.

In those days, checkers had to manually enter the cost of each item into the cash register. They had to remember the prices or visually find it on the packaging: no computers or swiping barcodes. It was a tedious job, best suited for an accomplished accountant with the patience of Job and the accuracy of a modern computer. A mistake took precious time to correct, and there were always impatient people waiting.

As each item was tallied, a bag boy bagged it. When a paper bag was full, he placed it carefully into a waiting empty cart. Waiting to help us push the cars to our transportation were four sturdy-looking young men. When my cart was finally emptied, tallied, and bagged, the exhausted checker handed *Mamá* a register list that stretched from hand to the floor and back again. I noticed a thin sheen of sweat on the checker's brow. She delicately wiped her forehead with a flowery white kerchief she'd removed from the pocket of her red cotton checker's apron. This was the moment for my sisters to shine. *Mamá* handed them the bill and together they checked for accuracy and to determine if our weekly check would cover the total tallied. Their collaboration took a few minutes. First, they checked the list for errant items *Mamá* hadn't purchased. *Mamá* never trusted it wouldn't happen. It was a cursory inspection, of course. Raquel was quicker than a whip, and Dolores had the memory of an elephant; together they made quick work of their task. They were next instructed to compare the two totals: the figure on the check and the one at the end of the grocery bill.

This was the stage in grocery shopping I hated most. You see, if the check total was insufficient to cover the total expenditure—and it happened on a few occasions—*Mamá* had to determine what she could and could not do without. She would quickly pick through the bags in the carts, looking for things we could do without and handing them to me to hand to the checker. As this was happening, the checker subtracted each item separately and gave us a running total until the total was under the grand sum of the check.

Then, *Mamá*, with a glance, would instruct me to reshelf the culled items. I found this task embarrassing, frustrating, and difficult. I had to run all over the store, looking for the exact spot where a particular item had been found. When I couldn't find the right place, I would just shelve it wherever I found room. Finding canned soup in the cooler with the milk couldn't have made the manager happy.

However, on this occasion, we were lucky. The check was more than sufficient, and Raquel gave *Mamá* an affirmative nod and returned it to her. *Mamá* then proudly signed it and handed it to the checker lady and waited. The fact we had earned enough money to buy groceries for the next week or two always made *Mamá* proud. To say she liked paying her own way was an understatement. The fact we only needed food assistance a couple times over all those years meant a lot to her. She was in a foreign country of which she knew little, and we were not only holding our own, we were being competitive: that was a badge of high honor to her. I think it reaffirmed her belief in our intelligence, character, and strong work ethic. She was confident that our belief in ourselves and our willingness to persevere the midst of hard times would be the key to our ultimate success. And she couldn't have been more right.

But this time there was a different problem. When *Mamá* handed the checker her check, the lady looked at it for a moment and handed it back to *Mamá*.

"I'm sorry, ma'am," she said, with a delicate sheen of perspiration still showing on her brow, "but we don't take two-party checks." *Mamá* looked quizzically at Raquel.

"*¿Qué dice?*" she asked.

"*Un momento, Mamá*," Raquel said. And, turning to the checker, "I'm sorry ma'am, what is a two-party check?" she inquired.

"Well, you're holding one in your hand, young lady," she said, with her lips pursed and her sharp chin jutting out arrogantly. After checking four carts of groceries, she probably felt she was overdue a cigarette or two. But she could see that explanation was insufficient. With hands on her skinny hips, she expelled a deep and exasperated sigh. I looked around to see if someone had let the air out of a car tire.

"A two-party check is made out to someone by another person that only the person it is made out to can cash. Since that check isn't made out to this store, we can't cash it."

"So then how do we pay for the groceries?" Raquel asked.

"Well, you can write me a personal check from your personal bank account or just take the check to your bank and they will cash it for you. Then you can bring the cash back here and pay for the groceries," she said, and smiled crookedly. Her expression said, "Are you people ignorant or something?" This was the first time any of us had heard of this two-party check thing, and it took Raquel a few minutes to explain it to *Mamá*. As *Mamá* listened, the strangest look came across her face. I'm not sure she fully grasped the concept of this two-party check thing Raquel was explaining, but she must have understood enough: to the grocery store, the check was no good.

Mamá waived the why/goodbye with a slight but meaningful hand gesture.

Still, she was faced with an interesting dilemma. I'd seen this look before: she was feeling a bit put out and somewhat incredulous. Now we had two women feeling similar emotions. *Mamá* had to say something, but should she respond in such a way that might be construed as negative or disrespectful? That was simply not her style. *Mamá* was thinking.

First and foremost, I'm sure *Mamá* wanted to ask the checker to stop for a moment—for it would not take much longer than that—to figure out who she was talking to. Any deaf, dumb, and blind mutton-head could see we were migrant laborers. We were darkly tanned, simply dressed in workers' clothes, not coiffured or perfumed, but still clean, neat, and tidy. It didn't take a genius to see we lived on the land: a hand-to-mouth existence. The idea we had enough money to put in a bank was about as ludicrous as expecting the bag boys to load our groceries into our waiting white Rolls Royce. *Mamá*'s face displayed humor with a hint of indignation. And second, all concerns of two-party checks aside, what she really wanted to say was, "Lady, the ice cream is melting."

When that funny look turned to a wily smile, I knew she was about to move into her action phase. The situation felt like a chess match and the checker lady was saying, "It's your move," as she looked at *Mamá* impatiently. I could hear the faint tapping of a hard-soled shoe on a polished linoleum floor. We looked at *Mamá,* waiting for her response. Raquel, Dolores, and I tensed and looked at each other, hoping someone had a solution. None of us did.

Then *Mamá* turned to Raquel and asked her to explain to the checker lady that we didn't have a bank account, but it was all right because she was sure the grocery store at the other end of town would cash a two-party check with no questions asked. Our eyes got as big as corn tortillas as we anticipated the lady's reaction. Raquel, unwilling to look the checker lady in the eye, translated as concisely as possible while we braced for a run for the door. I expected the checker lady to protest, at least, but she was as stunned as we were. She stumbled over her thick, dry tongue, and although I was sure she'd said something, no discernible words passed her lips.

Then *Mamá* folded the two-party check, opened her purse, and adroitly dropped it in. Above the deafening silence, I heard her purse snap shut with a loud click, like a coin being dropped in a blind man's tin cup. Then she said, "*Vámonos, chicos.*"

Raquel, Dolores, and I kept our eyes on the well-polished linoleum floor, and like dutiful ducklings, waddled behind *Mamá.* As I closed the door behind me, I turned to see the lady and the four bag boys looking at each other while six gallons of milk warmed, ice cream melted, and assorted vegetables wilted.

Five minutes later we were at the other end of town, loading four carts with groceries. But this time, wanting to avoid another uncomfortable stare down at the checkout counter, as we walked in, *Mamá* handed the check to Dolores and asked her to run it past the checker. She returned to report that two-party checks were gladly accepted. *Mamá* smiled and told us to grab some carts.

Personally, I wanted to find my brothers and run gleefully through the streets, but that bus had left town and I wasn't on it. *Mamá* had me where she wanted me.

Dirty Mexican

My elbows, knees, and knuckles
Were rough,
Dark, and calloused:
Dirty looking…
And my neck a blotchy brown.

"Has he ever heard of soap?"

No matter how hard I scrubbed,
Washrag, soap, or brush,
They remained dark and rough.
Yes, I guess I looked dirty…
But what else could I do?

"He smells too."

And at school
I kept my hands in my pockets—
As much as I could.
But that wasn't always possible.
I knew they noticed.
I heard the whispers.

"Jeez, he's dirty!"

DIRTY MEXICAN

But I wasn't.
I bathed like they did.
But the years of
Working in the dirt
Left rough, brown discolorations
That soap could not remove.

"I wish he'd shower!"

I'd scrub myself
Until I bled red,
And used bleach,
Until my skin burned…
To no avail.
Before and after school
I was in the fields,
No time to heal.

"We're not sitting next to him!"

Years later,
Long after I'd left the fields,
The rough, brown skin
And blotchy neck cleared.
But the echoes of
Their opinions of who
And what I was
Has never left me.

DIRTY MEXICAN

On occasion,
Not as often as before,
At the end of a day
In the garden
Or working on the car,
I look at my hands
And remember
I can still hear their condemnations…

Dirty Mexican.

What Did I Say?

You sat beside me
In the next row.
You wore frilly, lacy dresses:
Sometimes pink and
Sometimes blue.
I remember chestnut hair,
Friendly eyes,
And a pretty smile.
And we talked sometimes at lunch.
When Valentine's Day came
I gave you a card—a big red heart.
Do you love me—yes or no?
Are you my friend?
I want to know.

You crumpled it up
And threw it away.
"My parents won't let me take
Things from Mexicans," you said,
As you walked away.
And I slipped behind a shadow
Of embarrassment and sorrow.

What did I do?
What did I say?
Whom did I betray?
It didn't seem fair,
You didn't care,
As I quietly walked away.

We were on the same baseball team.
I played shortstop.
You played first.
We played basketball
And then flag football.
We spent time together
After school…until
You asked some friends
To walk to the Cozy Corner Grocery
With you for a Coke,
And I stood there alone,
Waiting to be invited,
But wasn't.
You walked by
Like I didn't exist.

What did I do?
What did I say?
Whom did I betray?
It didn't seem fair,
You didn't care,
As I quietly walked away.

WHAT DID I SAY?

We entered the classroom:
Miguel and I.
We sat in the front two desks.
We were proud.
There was so much to learn,
So much we wanted to know.
Our chance to move from
Dirt floors to chandeliers:
From the harshness of the fields
To the hope and promise…
The future safety
Intellect can wield.

With little tack,
And a bony index finger
Of your right hand
I think it was,
You motioned to the back.
Who would think
A finger could be so powerful.
We went from promise
To regret
With the pointing of a finger.
I looked into your eyes,
I saw no compromise.
I didn't have to ask.
By now, I knew the reasons why.
It had happened before…
But I had hoped you would be different.

WHAT DID I SAY?

I looked at Miguel,
He looked at me.
We understood the rules:
The unwritten ones,
And did as we were told,
But it was so cold.
Not the desk,
Or your finger,
It was your hardened, bigot soul.

What did I do?
What did I say?
Whom did I betray?
It didn't seem fair,
You didn't care,
As I quietly walked away.

I was walking home from
Baseball practice:
Four miles long it was.
And it was raining and I was cold…when
You stopped your car
And offered me a ride.
What a treat, I thought,
You were older,
More mature,
Had more money
And drove a shiny car.

WHAT DID I SAY?

When you let me out
I smiled and thanked you…
It was then I heard you say,
"I always try and
Give greasy spicks a ride."

What did I do?
What did I say?
Whom did I betray?
It didn't seem fair,
You didn't care,
As I quietly walked away.

You asked me to come home with you.
We could play catch,
Ride bicycles,
Throw the football,
And maybe watch television
With your family.
As I walked in,
You introduced me to your mother
And the first thing she said to me was
I need to wash my hair.
I shyly smiled and wondered why,
But I didn't protest.
I wanted desperately to stay,
And fit in.
You looked embarrassed
As she led me to the sink.

WHAT DID I SAY?

What did I do?
What did I say?
Whom did I betray?
It didn't seem fair,
You didn't care,
As I quietly walked away.

What did I say?

The White Boy

Memory is a fluid thing, even when it's young. Throw in emotions and the passing of seasons, and it flows like a meandering river through the light and dark places of my mind. At some point in the passing of time, you begin to question the memories: what was said and by whom, and even the place in time. But even after many years, I don't question the eyes. They seem indelibly etched in the memory of a ten-year-old Mexican boy: the eyes of the hungry white boy who came to dinner one balmy summer evening and stayed a few months. I remember the desperation I saw in those eyes. Sometimes, late in the evening when I'm reading, I look out the darkened window beside my bed and can still see their pale blueness reflecting back at me. I can still feel them. Hungry eyes never leave you.

It was a Saturday, early evening, and for the moment, all was finally settled: all had been forgiven. Not that the day had started out that way, or that forgiveness had been on our minds. A blistering sun had hung low overhead all week. All that summer. And our frenetic work in the field had worn us down to our basic elements, while the sun had baked us until we were indistinguishable from the dry, brown dirt we knelt in.

Mercifully, the sun was in retreat that evening, I recall, making its way across the Skagit River and down the western horizon. For a moment, the orange, fiery orb lingered over a white farmhouse and red barn that lay in a curious crook beside the river. Then, the sun gave up on us and the evening became pleasantly balmy.

For a long week, the farmer had us working from sunup

to sundown in the massive north field about ten minutes from the camp, along the riverbank. The summer had been an exceptionally hot one, and the strawberries were all ripening at the same time. The farmer knew if the berries weren't picked quickly, they would shrivel up and he would lose a lot of money. Other than a few head of cattle he raised and sold, strawberries were his only crop that year, and now his back was up against the barn door. So, at the beginning of the week, he told Salvador, the camp foreman, if we finished the field by Friday, he would throw us a camp party and give us a few days off. He said he would provide all the Olympia beer the men could drink and hamburgers, hot dogs, and chicken the women could barbecue. We didn't hear benevolence in the farmer's offer: it was desperation, pure and simple. But desperation or benevolence mattered little to us. For people accustomed to dirt in our beans and the harshness of summer heat on our backs, it sounded like a festival. It was something to hope for, and to a child, that can mean the difference between joy and despair. All the families in the camp decided they would work extra hard, long into the summer evenings, to finish by Friday.

We worked like dogs all week, and by early evening on Friday we found ourselves at least four hours short of finishing the huge field. When it got too dark to see the strawberries, we had to quit. As we climbed back into the flatbed truck, we could see the farmer talking to Salvador in the unfinished field, kicking the soft dirt with his boot, hands deep in his front pockets.

We knew little about the farmer. He appeared to be in his mid-fifties, tall and lean. He always wore a baseball cap with the International Harvester logo on the front, a white

T-shirt, blue jeans, and Red Wing work boots. No one talked disparagingly about him, not openly anyway. Because his demands were always channeled through Salvador, we never dealt with him directly. Whether in the fields or in camp, he never acknowledged us. He seemed to look through us. It was like we were ghosts to him. Not that we cared. He was a ghost to us as well. What I know of him now, from the vantage point of over fifty years of passing seasons and dirt beneath my feet, is that he provided better housing for his cattle than he did for the Mexicans who worked for him. What that said about him may be open for interpretation, but not by me.

As the farmer talked, Salvador removed his straw hat and wiped the sweat from his brown with the red bandana always found around his neck. Then, he nervously wiped sweat from the inside of his hat, held in his hands. He was a tall man for a Mexican and could look the farmer eye to eye, but didn't. Instead, he looked into his straw hat and watched the farmer kick the dirt as they talked. The farmer's body language said all we needed to know about how he felt about us not finishing the field. It was a strange dance we were watching, between two tough men, both used to getting what they wanted. The farmer, knowing there was still a lot of work to be done, didn't want to display his anger and risk alienating those he needed most. Salvador, his trusted foreman, knowing how hard we'd worked all week, didn't want to be seen siding with the farmer and not appreciating our efforts and sacrifice. Then, Salvador put his hat back on his head, said something to the farmer, nodded affirmatively, squared his brown shoulders, and returned to the truck. The farmer was left alone, nervously contemplating the next day, watching the light disappear from the field.

Salvador must have realized his delicate position as he neared the truck. He wanted to please the disappointed farmer but be respectful of *Mamá*, a woman few people dared cross words with. When he got to us, he cautiously removed his hat and wiped his brown again. He quickly reassured *Mamá* that as long as we finished the field by Saturday at noon, the party was still on. *Mamá* confidently assured him that would not be a problem. I wondered how she could be so certain, but on second thought, I knew *Mamá* had spent her entire life in the fields and if she thought we could finish by noon, who was I to second-guess her? Salvador must have come to the same conclusion because he didn't argue or question. He smiled, nodded respectfully, and drove us back to camp.

As the truck drove out of the field, I looked back at what I could see of the unfinished field and wondered if I could survive another day, short as it might be, in the kind of heat we'd experienced that day. In the dusk and dust of the day that remained, we traveled back to camp, exhausted from one of the longest days I could remember. Even at my young age, unfortunately, I could remember more than a few.

Saturday started early and with little time for breakfast. *Mamá* told us there would be plenty to eat when the work was done. That did little to assuage my hunger and grumbling stomach as we loaded onto the farmer's flatbed truck at eight. *Mamá* pushed us hard all morning and, true to her prediction, it was closing in on noon when we were finishing our last rows. The sun was directly above us and no less formidable than the previous day. I was thankful for the short day.

You can't imagine the joy I felt when I saw *Mamá* finish her row, then double back on mine to help me. *Mamá* was a picking machine, her hands, delicately but swiftly, flying over the strawberry bushes, always finishing ahead of us, and when she did, she could be counted on to double back onto our row and help us. That way, she could keep us close to her. From experience, I knew that was important to her. I think she knew how seeing her coming down our row encouraged us. It would have been so easy—at the end of a long day, looking down a strawberry row that seemed miles long—to give up. And the scorching sun worked to destroy what little self-discipline we had as children. I vividly recall, on numerous occasions, feeling like sitting down, putting my head in my lap, giving up, and crying in defeat, until I saw *Mamá* coming down my row. She always rekindled my resolve.

When we completed our rows, we gathered our flats and turned them into the checker who waited in the shade of a twenty-by-twenty beige tarp where the berry flats were ready for pickup by the farmer. I stood beside *Mamá* and looked at the Sanchez, Garcia, and Hernandez families, all waiting to check in their flats. At the head of each family stood a father with a deeply creased bronze face, thick callused hands, wearing a farmer's straw hat. It felt strangely uncomfortable to me that at the head of the Ledesma family was only *Mamá*. And although I remember feeling she had to be the most courageous woman in the world, it still made me feel inexplicably anxious. She and *Papá* had separated a few years earlier, and that meant we had to leave the small farm we loved. It had to have taken us years of hard work and savings to finally be able to put a down payment on the small thirty-acre farm that *Mamá* walked away from. And so here was *Mamá*, with nine of us in tow, working in a man's world, trying her darnedest to keep us fed, together, and safe. But after leaving the farm and *Papá*, I would never feel safe again. I carried that feeling deep into adulthood. Dreams of being somewhere strange and trying in vain to find my way home, always laced with fear and anguish, have followed me all my life. But strangely enough, during times when I feel most unsafe, it has always been *Mamá's* image that's helped soothe me, not *Papá's*.

Mamá handed the checker our tickets as Juan and Enrique stacked twenty full flats, the product of our last two hours of picking, under the beige tarp. He slowly counted what we'd gathered and began punching the tickets that would later be turned in for pay. The last hour had been a flurry of nimble hands as we picked with the determination of an evening party waiting. When the checker handed *Mamá* back the punched tickets, she put them in her front pocket and told us to get in the truck. Although it was only about noon, it had already been a long day. We finished about the time *Mamá* said we would, but had paid a high price. We were completely spent. Our knees, backs, and necks ached from constant kneeling, crouching, bending, and straightening. Every ounce of energy was gone, and we were hot, hungry, dirty, and sweaty. My throat was beginning to close, my eyes were dirt dry, and my brain felt like it was swelling from the heat. The end of any work day was usually the cause for some elation. Not this time. The ride back to camp was a somber affair. As I looked at my brothers and sisters, I could see the same exhaustion in their eyes I felt in my body. None of us had any inclination toward conversation.

When we got back to our cabins, *Mamá* handed us clean jeans, underwear, socks, and T-shirts, and told us to head for the showers. Since we were not the only ones taking showers, when I got there, I had to wait for thirty minutes. By the time

I got in, the hot water was gone, not that I cared. I stood under the streaming cold water and soaped up three times before I began to feel clean. I blew brown, dirty snot out of my nose, shampooed the dirt out of my hair twice, and spit grit out of my mouth. I didn't care who was waiting in line; I was going to saturate and hydrate my skin and let the water soak deep into my vital organs, until I felt closer to the cool river than the dry dirt I'd been in all morning. When we had all taken our showers and put on clean clothes, we sat around the table in *Mamá's* cabin and waited patiently as she made bean burritos to hold us until the party. We drank purple Kool-Aid and ate a small but satisfying meal. Our work was done, but *Mamá's* continued. She had to be at least as tired as we were, but there she was, taking care of us and still in the kitchen, stoking the fire and preparing for the party. It appeared as if her work was never finished. Later in life, I inquired about this perception, and her answer surprised me. It shouldn't have. She said she really didn't feel free to think about herself or even take a relaxing breath until we had all left home, and much to her consternation she still worries about us.

As *Mamá* boiled pinto beans that had soaked overnight in a large, deep kettle and made tortillas for the party, my brothers disappeared. The girls stayed behind to help. I sat on the wood steps of our cabin and finally felt something akin to joy. No, we didn't have anything and our lives didn't appear to be going anywhere, but I was still elated. I was so relieved to be out of the sun-scorched fields, showered, and in clean clothes, that for a moment, I permitted myself to feel good. It's like when you hurt yourself and the pain finally ceases. The way you look at life changes.

Mamá ladled the beans into a large black cast-iron pan, added salt and lard, and mashed them, making refried beans. At the same time, Raquel and Dolores rolled out the dough for tortillas, and together they cooked them on the broad surface of the woodstove. The men were barbecuing the meat on the spits between the first and second row of cabins, drinking beer, and talking about how good life was. They had work, shelter, money coming in, and soon, their bellies would be full. And when the cold beer quenched their immense thirst, what else could they ask for? As I sat, recording these images and listening to the gaiety around me, the incongruity of what I was seeing, hearing, and feeling was not lost on me, even at ten. Here we were, at the bottom of society's economic and social ladder, working in subhuman, dangerous conditions, in pesticide-saturated fields. And still, we talked of life being good. But I had to smile, at least for the moment. I was thanking God for small favors and trying to enjoy what little I had to feel good about. I understood that feeling, momentary and fleeting as it was, had to do with the fact that there was nothing more I could want.

The Burlington camp was situated beside the Skagit River, on the north side of the bridge separating Mount Vernon and Burlington. A gravel road ran parallel to the river and in front of the camp. Now that the sun was down, a delicate, cool breeze off the river fanned the camp, and spirits were high. *Mamá* was sitting with her *comadres*, talking and dishing food to the men and children. Cigarette smoke was swirling pungently around the table of old men talking, playing cards, and drinking beer. I was sitting at a picnic table consumed with getting enough food to satisfy my longing for a full belly, which was the only security readily available to me.

I was eating—and ever vigilant. Being vigilant came with the migrant lifestyle. As children, we had seen and experienced more than children should ever be allowed to see or experience. It gave birth to the invasive feeling we were never safe.

I suddenly noticed something unusual. A white boy, maybe a few years older than I, walking slowly along the gravel road, approaching camp. When I noticed him, he was about seventy-five yards from us. As he neared, I could see him intently watching the boisterous Mexican camp. When he got directly across from us, he stopped and stood, silent and alone. I looked up and down the road for a broken-down car, or maybe his parents following behind, but from what I didn't see, I knew he was alone. He stood for the longest minute with his hands in his front pockets. He repeatedly looked down at his feet and then back at us. He looked up and down the road and then back to us. He seemed to be saying something. Maybe he was reassuring us he was alone and posed no threat. Maybe he was just alone and lost. One thing for sure was the resolve I saw in his face to not take one step farther up or down that road, away from the camp. His shoulders sagged under the weight of something I innately understood: defeat. He looked like I often felt at the end of a long day in the fields: like I couldn't go one more step. Like giving up.

Enrique and Juan were eating, sitting at the end of the table closest to the road and the boy. They had been watching him too. Both looked to *Mamá* and I saw her nod. Juan said something to Enrique and they got up together. In their younger days, they seemed to do everything in unison.

No one else in the camp moved, but many had noticed the white boy standing beside the gravel road. There was some murmuring among some families, but no one seemed exactly sure of the protocol if a white boy should come wandering into a Mexican labor camp. I had never seen any rules to cover such an odd event written anywhere in the camp literature. Not that there was any camp literature.

So I wasn't sure what *Mamá* had in mind when she nodded to my older brothers. They seemed to understand perfectly, however, because they immediately left their plates, got up, and walked toward the white boy. And as they did, everyone in the camp went back to what they were doing. They must have thought whatever needed to be done about the white boy standing on the side of the road would be taken care of by Juan and Enrique.

And he stayed, not moving an inch, as Juan and Enrique approached him. If you didn't know us, you might have thought the probability of conflict was high. He was no taller than Juan or Enrique and possibly about the same age, but decidedly thinner. Yes, violence was a way of life in the camps. Maybe I half expected a fight to break out. I had no idea what those two were up to, but I should have known. When Juan got to the boy, he stretched his arm out and opened his brown hand. For a moment, the boy wasn't sure what to do. When he understood what Juan was doing, he timidly reached out and shook Juan's hand. I watched them talk for a minute or so. Then, with Juan leading the way and Enrique following behind the white boy, they walked back into camp. I took a quick glance at *Mamá*. There was a kind smile on her face. Nothing really obvious, but it was there. Juan led the boy to *Mamá* and a short discussion ensued.

When the boy passed me, I noticed he was dressed in ragged, dirty clothes. He wore a gray T-shirt that looked like it might have, at one time, been white. His jeans had holes in both knees and were help up at the waist with a thin, worn, brown leather belt cinched at the last hole. His jeans were at least two sizes too big for him. If they were his, it was obvious he hadn't had a decent meal in a very long time. He had a dirty face, and tear streaks interrupted dirt caked on his cheeks. And I thought we were poor, I said to myself. Later in life, from a different vantage point, I remember coming upon emaciated stray dogs in camp that looked better kept and fed than that boy. And I think the only thing on his mind that evening was food. Maybe he was hoping for shelter and a safe night's sleep as well, but filling his sunken belly had to be in the forefront of his mind. There was no reason he should have expected he would get any of it in the camp among a bunch of Mexicans, but he had been desperate enough to find out.

After talking to Juan a few moments, *Mamá* waved the boy to her and motioned for him to grab one of the paper plates. She took it from him and filled it with refried beans, a hamburger, barbecued chicken, Spanish rice, and a fistful of warm tortillas. She then told the boys to sit him next to them and make sure he was safe and had enough to eat. Juan and Enrique led him back past me, to the end of the table, where their plates still sat. They sat him between them and commenced eating. Juan quickly noticed the boy looking down at his wonderful plate of food with a bit of confusion.

"I don't have a spoon or a fork," the boy said shyly.

"We don't need them," Juan reassured him. "We eat like this." He tore a tortilla in half and scooped the food up. The chicken, Juan told him, he would need to eat with his fingers. It didn't take the boy long to figure it out, and when next I looked, he had eaten every bit of the food *Mamá* had placed on his plate. The only thing left on his plate were chicken bones. Hunger was excellent motivation for quick learning. He didn't have to ask for another helping. Enrique, who had been watching him closely, grabbed his plate and returned it to *Mamá*. *Mamá* smiled broadly, like a mother does when she sees her child satisfied, said something that made Enrique laugh, and filled it up again. The boy ate a second and then started on a third before he began to slow down. He seemed to have a bottomless pit in him because he finished more than a dozen tortillas before pausing. When he finally finished, he had time to take stock of where he was. I watched him as he looked around with eyes as big as harvest moons. I could tell he was feeling a lot of things, but hunger was not one of them. His belt might have had to be let out one inch. I could hear Juan and Enrique chatting with him, and after about thirty minutes, all three got up and walked back to where *Mamá* was sitting. With *Mamá*, they talked for a while, and again with a wave of her hand, she dismissed them. They walked away in the direction of our cabins. I didn't see the three of them again until we gathered in our cabin at the end of a long night of partying.

When I finally couldn't stand not knowing a minute longer, I found *Mamá* and asked her about the white boy. She said she had no idea who he was.

"What did he want?" I asked her. She said he had told her he hadn't eaten in days and was alone. "That was all I needed to hear," she said.

"So what happens now?" I asked.

"He has no place to live so I told him he was welcome to stay with us until he finds a place to stay. I told him if he wanted a job, he would work with us."

"And what then?" I asked.

"Well, when he's ready to make it on his own, he can leave, but until then, I told him he was safe with us."

"Really?" I said, incredulous.

"*M'ijo*, you don't turn away a hungry, homeless child, regardless of color. Hunger and homelessness has no color, just a need that has to be met, and that's where we are. That's our way.

"Why don't any of the other families do anything to help the boy, *Mamá*?" I inquired, thinking it strange none of them stepped forward or even said anything.

"*M'ijo*, it's not important what other people do or don't do in these times. It's only important that we did something. He is now part of our family until it's his time to leave, like someday it will be your time to leave."

"I hope it's never my time to leave, *Mamá*."

Mamá just smiled and lit another Marlboro.

"Everybody leaves eventually, *M'ijo*. It's all about growing older and stronger and being ready." She smiled and blew smoke into the cool night air.

"I'm not ever leaving, *Mamá*!" I said emphatically. She smiled. Her eyes sparkled love as she continued to blow smoke into the cool evening air.

When *Mamá* sent word around that it was time for us to go to bed, it was already late. Usually, she wanted to know we were safe in bed long before she retired, but she let us stay up since we had a few days off. As I was readying for bed, Juan, Enrique, and the white boy entered the cabin. The first thing I noticed was this white boy looked altogether different from the one I'd seen standing beside the road a few hours earlier. He had showered and was wearing either Juan's or Enrique's extra clothes. He had pale blue eyes and dark blond hair. And it wasn't simply that he was clean, had on clean clothes, and had a belly full of good food. He stood erect, his shoulders were back, his eyes gleamed, and he had the biggest smile I can remember ever seeing on a ruddy, red-scrubbed face. I was looking at the miraculous transformation when *Mamá* walked in. She gave him an approving smile. In the midst of a dirty environment, cleanliness was an obsession with her. I recall her saying a hundred times, "We may be poor but that doesn't mean we can't be clean." Upon inspection, he passed.

She instructed Juan and Enrique that as long as the boy was with us, they were to accompany him wherever they went. She took mothering seriously. I think she wanted to make sure the boy understood our commitment to him.

Since there were only four bunks in the cabin, the boy would have to share a bunk. Juan was thirteen and Enrique, twelve: too big to share a small bunk. That left me, going on eleven, and Mario, who was nine. Mario was the smallest, so the boy bunked with him, at least until Salvador could find an extra bunk. Not that the boy cared. I think he just felt fortunate to have a roof over his head and a warm bed to sleep in.

Before the light was turned off, Juan finally introduced us to our new brother. The boy told us his name was Joseph but could not remember the last time anyone called him that. He asked us to call him Joey.

Since none of us had ever spent any close-up time with white people, and considering the negative stories we grew up hearing about them, I'm sure we all had our doubts. Not *Mamá*. She had a family to take care of and had little time or energy for speculating on odds. He would either make it or move on.

As the days came and went, I watched Joey closely from afar. Since he was older than me, he spent his time between Juan and Enrique. In the fields, neither of them would permit Joey to outwork them, or, away from the fields, outplay them. That meant both paid more attention to their work ethic and worked harder, to prove to anyone watching that Mexicans were superior to whites when it came to working in the fields or playing games. What I saw of Joey that summer convinced me we had possibly misjudged the whites. Joey kept his head down and hands moving with the diligence and dexterity of a poor Mexican, fearful of where his next meal was coming from. And whether Juan or Enrique outworked or outplayed Joey or not depended on who you talked to.

But what ultimately impressed me most about Joey was his adoration of *Mamá*. He didn't have to understand Spanish, nor did she need to speak English, for him to know what she needed at any time. If she looked at the dwindling wood pile beside the woodstove, he went searching for the axe and, before she could say a word, he was bringing in an armload of chopped wood. If she needed water, he was grabbing the aluminum pail and walking out the door.

Mamá never had to ask him to do anything because he anticipated her every need and was usually a step ahead of her. On occasion—a few times that summer, after a long day in the fields, during dinner—when he looked at *Mamá*, I saw tears in his eyes. If anyone else noticed, no one mentioned it. I quietly began to view *Mamá* from the unexpected vantage point of a white stranger, and it made me feel I hadn't really known this Mexican woman I called *Mamá*. Watching her dedication to him and his adoration of her began to change how I viewed *Mamá*, our family, and ultimately, white people. In the ensuing weeks and months, we ended up getting pretty close to Joey. He stayed with us for the rest of the summer and into the fall. At the end of each week, when *Mamá* got paid, he got whatever he earned. *Mamá* would not hear of him paying for anything. She fed and clothed him as if he were one of us. We understood Joey could keep all he earned, but it never crossed our minds to ask why we couldn't. Without asking, we knew it took the family's cumulative efforts to sustain us. We never complained.

During this time, I continued to ponder what *Mamá* had done. At one point, I remember asking her about being poor and how we could just take in a stranger. I told her I understood our obligation to feed someone who came to us hungry, but making them part of our already large family seemed an odd thing to do when we had so little. She said, "*M'ijo*, we're not poor. Yes, we don't have much money and we don't own anything. But poor are those who don't have family. As long as we're together, we're as rich an anyone."

"*Si, Mamá*," I said, smiling. It felt better knowing we weren't really poor.

I still had many questions about how he ended up standing alone, beside the road in front of our camp. And years later, I recall quizzing *Mamá* about him, and she told me she ever asked and never knew. I guess it hadn't been important to her. But she always talked with no little pride in being able to help him. I understood it was a lesson she wanted us all to learn.

Nothing *Mamá* did that fateful summer should have surprised me. I've never met a woman, rich or poor, in possession of such uniquely compassionate qualities. At five foot eight, she might have been a little taller than most women of her time, but her willingness to love and care for those less fortunate, for broken and lost children, set her well apart from the rest.

As things turned out, it was a good summer. Joey was a great diversion for us all. Watching him work hard, grow, and appreciate his new temporary family was exactly what we, and he, needed. When the harvest was done and the cool fall evenings began to put color on the leaves, it was time for us to return to Outlook, east of the mountains, where we rented a house. Joey had gained a good ten pounds and sported a healthy tan, a willing smile, and a mischievous sense of humor, which he needed to keep up with us. And although *Mamá* assured him he was welcome to live with us as long as he wanted, he decided to stay in the Skagit Valley. We never saw or heard from him again, and to this day, I have no idea what became of him. That's not to say I haven't thought about him. I often wondered if he found a home and was safe. I often wondered if he remembered us as fondly, as I still remember him. I want to believe he became something meaningful. And when I remember him through *Mamá's* eyes and actions, he already was someone wonderful.

This was the first time I experienced *Mamá* taking in a white boy, but not the last. She did it at least two or three more times. With the wave of her hand, she changed their lives. With the power of her compassionate heart, she changed ours.

Hooray for Handsome Chavelo

I saw you there,
In a faded photograph
Of black and white—standing tall,
Behind a gaggle of us brown-haired,
Bronze-skinned *hermanos y hermanas.*

The sun was orange,
The shadows long,
The day's work was all but done.

Your bony chest was out.
The Kodak Brownie caught
A white, toothy smile
Cross your face:
A show of confidence saying
You knew,
You knew you had it—what it took to conquer
And rise above our world of
Tattered, dirty clothes,
Poverty and violence:
Our dilapidated present,
To an improbable future.

But you weren't like the rest of us.
Dreamers—we were.
Dreamers with little but our dreams
To feed the hunger that gnawed
In our extended bellies,
And put to sleep
Our weary, tired souls.

No—not a dreamer were you,
But a thinker,
A maker,
And a doer.

You knew you could do it all,
Didn't you?
Every day, you knew you could think
And maneuver your way
Through poverty's stench
And decay.

Hooray for handsome Chavelo:
Light of skin,
Fair of hair,
Tall and straight,
The good life shining like
The noonday sun
In your eyes.

HOORAY FOR HANDSOME CHAVELO

And you escaped,
Didn't you:
The backbreaking,
Muscle-aching,
Sun-scorching
Dirty work
That was left
To the lot of us?

You'd had your share
And it was enough
To last you a lifetime,
Maybe more,
You were sure.

And us…you left behind
To feed our dreams
With pinto beans,
In dismay and disarray,
With only photographs
And fading memories
In black and white,
Of a time when we felt right.

Graduation—then summer came.
It was then you went
To town—I think it was,
Disappearing into the balmy night.
While your empty bed
Collected the moonlight

HOORAY FOR HANDSOME CHAVELO

That peeked through
Dusty, worn drapes
That mother made
When the rains came
And washed away
All thoughts of labor.

We waited for you there.
We looked down the long
Undulations of a potholed driveway,
And into the void
That held our emptiness like
An unrequited prayer.

Neither God
Nor the empty night
Nor the void that kept our hopes
Answered our calls.

The days went by,
Then back to school.
You called from somewhere—
Beyond the driveway,
Sugar beets, asparagus,
And alfalfa fields.
And we who loved you
Waited—anxiously,
Contemplated a quick return
That never came.

First the military,
Then California, *Mamá* said.
Marriage, work, and family kept you busy.
You visited
On occasion,
But never stayed.
Not the same.

Hooray for handsome Chavelo:
Light of skin,
Fair of hair,
Tall and straight,
The good life shining like
The noonday sun
In your eyes.

What happened to handsome Chavelo,
Cheeky picture full of confidence,
When your youth,
And then your will,
Faded like the waning summer moon?
And there, you found yourself alone,
Alone among the gringos.

Did you think your thoughts
Were demands of playful gods,
And the universe waited on
And listened to you alone,
Or that dreams
Secured your happiness?

But no—instead,
The reality of life transpired
Between the lying down—of head
Full of plans and diagrams,
On soiled pillow—
And getting up
With desires still swirling
In the sky,
Like *agua sucia* down the drain.
Did you think wishes
Were whiskey, inebriating the gods
Who sent manna from Savanna
For the worthy,
Worthy of having
Sans the burden of the labor?

Did wishing make you *borracho*, drunk?
Too *borracho* to understand
The realities—stark,
Affecting us?
Smiles didn't bring tortillas
Nor laughter empanadas
For summer fiestas,
Bailes con dark skinned *novias*
Wearing colorfully embroidered cotton dresses
In cool evening breezes.

And then you found,
To your surprise,
When you awoke,
You had to face
Your life without the magic.
Oh, how tragic
To be on your own.

(*¿Y qué pasó hermano?*)
What happened to you?
To make you quit,
To come home
To roost or rest,
Or maybe die.
Too old to do
What once was easy
When you were young,
In black-and-whites
As the sun was setting
And shadows long,
The day's work all but done.

Too late for me
And for us.
Now too old to believe
In ethereal gods and fairytales,
And answered prayers
And mystic tales.

HOORAY FOR HANDSOME CHAVELO

HOORAY FOR HANDSOME CHAVELO

Too old to believe
In the benevolence of man,
The righteousness of good,
And the integrity of purpose.

So leave it to the young
Who know no better
That setting suns
Set for them,
And you,
And I,
And they,
And he,
And she…
It's all to be.
None can flee.

And I and we, we've left no faith:
'Twas lost on summer's eve
So many years ago.
It happened in a dream—
So surreal!

Where along the dusty road
Did you lose your way?
And did we our faith?
And does it matter anymore?

Hooray for handsome Chavelo,
Light of skin,
Fair of hair,
Tall and straight,
The good life shining like
The noonday sun
In your eyes.

Hooray for handsome Chavelo.

Just Sit Quietly—Part 1

(Freshman English)

It was a cool October morn
When we entered late:
Freshman English class,
Carlos Cruz and I.
We stood for a moment
Surveying the class,
Front to back,
Looking for desks,
A good place to sit,
Maybe a window seat
To watch the wind blow
Through the trees
That lined the sidewalk below.

The teacher looked up,
Then simply pointed
To the back.
Carlos nudged me.
I saw the empty desks
In the back.
I sighed,
Didn't have to wonder why.

When roll was called
We didn't hear our names,
Carlos Cruz and I.
I raised my hand
To ask the teacher why.
He didn't deny.

"Yes, you're in the right class.
Just sit quietly," he spoke, defiantly.

I looked at Carlos—
He looked down at his hands,
Calloused and dark,
As if an answer might be found there,
But none was found there.

And when we looked around,
Everyone had a book
But we did not.
We looked at each other,
Carlos Cruz and I,
Wondering if he'd made a mistake.
Was he a flake?
Again, I raised my hand
To ask the reason why.

"*Just sit quietly,*" he spoke, defiantly.

"What the hell is going on, Carlos?" I whispered.
"Are you feeling paranoid? he asked.
"I am," I replied.

The bell rang—ending class.
When everyone was gone,
On my way out,
I stopped by the teacher's desk
And looked him in the eye
And asked the reason why.
We felt denied,
Carlos Cruz and I.

Yes, I know we're late,
Nothing we could do.
It's a family thing.
We need to work
But now we're here
And want to learn.

"You can stay,
But *just sit quietly*," he spoke, defiantly.
"That's my way.
Just sit quietly
Or be on your way."
"If I wanted to—*just sit quietly*,
As you say,
I could do it in the library,
Thank you very much!" I said,
And walked out.

I never returned
To Freshman English class.

The next day I made my way to the library.
I found a desk tucked in the back
Behind a long, tall shelf of books.
The 800 section, literature, I think,
And *just sat quietly*.

It was a cool October morn.

Just Sit Quietly—Part 2

(The Library)

"What are you doing here son—trying to hide,
Skipping class?" the librarian boldly inquired,
When she found me sitting quietly behind
A bookshelf in the back,
Long after the bell had rung.
She looked down at me
From over reading glasses.

"No, ma'am, just trying to read," I replied.

"You being smart with me, son?
You're in my library
And in my library
No one comes or goes without
Me knowing and approving," she said.
Still looking down at me,
But now more sternly
Over reading glasses,
With a sharp edge to her voice
That gave me fright.

"I didn't sneak in here, ma'am.
I would have asked permission
But when I walked in, you weren't here," I replied,
Intimidated and worried.

"Where are you supposed to be this period, son?"

"Freshman English, ma'am, room 209,
But things didn't go well.
It wasn't a pleasant experience."

"Oh, so now education is supposed
To be a pleasant experience, huh?
Well, let me tell you something,
It isn't always easy
And sometimes it's harder
Than we want,
But that's education, son.
If it was fun, it would be recess.
If you want it, you have
To be willing to pay the price."

"Oh, I'm not complaining
About education being hard, ma'am,
Or not being willing to pay the price.
I know about hard, ma'am.
Hard is living in rat-infested shacks
And working in dust-
Choked fields
In the blistering sun,
From sunup to sundown.
Compared to that,
Education is a piece of
Lemon meringue pie, ma'am.
I'm not trying to be disrespectful
But that's the truth
As I've experienced it, ma'am,"
I said, turning to look at some books,
Eyes brimming with tears.

"I concede your point, son,
But I still need to call your teacher.
What do you say about that?"

"Do as you wish, ma'am,
But it won't do any good.
He doesn't care who
Or where I am,
As long as I'm in the back.
Brown hands folded
And mouth shut.

We sat in the back,
Carlos Cruz and I.
When roll was read
Our names weren't called.
When papers were passed out
We didn't get any.
And when we asked the reason why,
Just sit quietly, was what he said—the teacher,
And bowed his head."

"When books were passed…" I said
"Let me guess—they didn't last!"
"How'd you guess?"
"I think I know the rest," she whispered,
Almost inaudibly.
And with her long index finger
With red painted nail,
She fixed her reading glasses right.

"I told him I wouldn't do it,
Just sit quietly—that is.
I told him if I wanted to
Just sit quietly,
I'd do so in the library.
He just smiled as I walked on by.
So here I am, ma'am."

"I see Hemingway, Fitzgerald,
Steinbeck, Buck, Hardy,
And all their friends, waiting for you.
What else do you need?"

"Nothing, ma'am.
I think I am home."

"Welcome to Freshman English, son.
Are you comfortable?
"Yes, ma'am. I'm getting that way."

Just sit quietly.

Slugger

Every childhood toy I remember playing with was made by my brother Juan.

When *Mamá* hit the road with nine of us in tow—soon after my *padres'* divorce—and for the next few years, we spent the harvest seasons in migrant camps from Monmouth, Oregon, to Sedro-Woolley, Washington. And since store-bought toys were out of reach for a family living hand to mouth, what Juan saw, he made with a seasoned wood-carver's precision.

Even though our winter rental wasn't far from the farm, the divorce was a world-titling shift. I was about nine when it happened. Leaving the farm left me worried and suffering from troubled sleep for years. I wondered what we were going to do without *Papá* and the safety of the home we'd worked so long to buy. I had stomachaches without origins and nightmares without meaning.

On the road, we spent every dollar we made on food and clothes. Life was about survival, and we all understood sacrifices had to be made. Although we had been poor on the farm, the idea and experience of poor took on a more insidious meaning on the road without *Papá's* protection and living in labor camp housing unfit for a farmer's dogs.

Francisco, around sixteen, was the oldest when we left the farm, Arturo the youngest at four. The rest of us fell in yearly increments somewhere in between. Chavelo, Manuel, and Maria were long gone before our time of separation and wanderings.

As a family on the road, if we wanted toys, it was understood we had to make our own. Not that it was a conversation I remember ever taking place between *Mamá* and us. It was pretty obvious to all of us. And when I say all of us, I specifically mean us boys. Since Raquel and Dolores were older, their sights were more on boys than dolls. And what Linda, a year younger than I, did for toys, I don't recall.

So that was when Juan, a few years older than I, started creating his masterpieces. Anything we wanted, he created out of scraps of wood he found along the way and in the labor camps. He used knives, small hand saws, sandpaper, nails, screws, rope, and scraps of leather to create whatever he imagined. He was magic with his hands. I was fascinated by what he could make with next to nothing.

Give him a few tools, and he could create sailboats, knives, and swords out of one-by-sixes; machine guns from old fence posts; M1 carbines and forty-five caliber handguns out of discarded two-by-fours; and bullets could be whittled from bits of wood.

Juan's talent emerged from necessity, but his real masterpiece was born out of his love of baseball and a chance encounter with the farmer's children on one sunny day in June.

It was a Monday morning when we woke to thunder rumbling angrily through the sky. And then, the dark clouds opened up and a hard, driving rain inundated the camp. The corrugated tin roof of the shack we slept in shuddered from the concussion of the thunder, and the driving rain made it sound like a snare drum. The heavy sounds reverberated through the cabin, becoming part of my dreams as I lay in the in-between world, neither asleep nor awake. I woke with the image of a sailboat tossed by a violent sea under dark clouds, deluged by a hard rain. The boat was in trouble. Half asleep, I wondered what we had done to make the sky so angry. I closed my eyes again. As I opened them, my dream fears melted, replaced by the familiar feeling of being lost. Since leaving the farm, I often awoke feeling lost and afraid.

I rolled from my stomach onto my back and pulled the covers over my head, listening for the news that always followed the sound of hard rain.

After a few tentative moments, I heard Salvador's knock on the cabin next door, followed by a short conversation. The conversation was muffled, but I knew the message. Salvador told *Mamá* what she already knew: work would be delayed until the rain stopped and the soil between the strawberry rows dried. That meant at least until noon and possibly longer. From the heavy, constant drum of rain, I knew it could be an all-day layoff. My brothers and I lingered for a few more minutes under the warm covers before deciding it was time to take advantage of some free time away from the fields. Regardless of the rain and the loss of a work day, we knew children throughout the camp were celebrating and readying to gather in small groups and run wild. Juan, Enrique, Mario, and I slipped our work jeans on and stood huddled together for a moment on the door's threshold, watching the rain fall and water form large puddles around the cabins. It looked like we were about to be swept off our flimsy moorings and go cascading down the Skagit River. The warmth of last night's fire was long gone and we were shivering. Although *Mamá's* cabin was only fifteen feet away, we knew we were in for a good soaking before we reached her door. Then, Enrique jumped and the rest of us followed.

Unlike ours, *Mamá's* cabin was warm with the smells of boiling pinto beans, coffee, and tortillas cooking on the woodstove. *Mamá* had always been an early riser. Before the activity of the day began, often before the sun was up, she could be found sitting at the table sipping Folgers coffee and smoking a Marlboro. She drank her coffee with cream and sugar when we had it. When we were on the road and without refrigeration, cream was not an option. She was not the kind of heavy smoker that had a cigarette in her mouth all day. Her downtime was her smoke time, and early morning was the prime opportunity to enjoy the only two vices I ever knew her to have. (The only vice that remained with her into her nineties was her coffee.)

In the time of our family's wanderings, *Mamá* became a contemplative woman who enjoyed her quiet time when she could get it. I've long suspected she took strength from these quiet moments, sitting alone, coffee in one hand, Marlboro in the other, pleading the fate of her children with a full heart to the empty space around her.

Then the sun would come up and bring her about as much as she could handle. Looking back, we kids had to be a large part of that "about as much as she could handle."

That Monday morning, we sat at the picnic table in her warm cabin and waited patiently for breakfast, chattering excitedly about what we were going to do with our free morning. *Mamá* had explained the rain delay: the morning would be ours.

Mamá said she didn't think the rain was going to stop anytime soon but to check back immediately when it did. Either way, when the sun was straight overhead, we should check back, if not for work, at least for lunch. Since none of us wore a watch, the sun was the only way we told time. In all my youth I cannot remember anyone owning, much less wearing, a watch. And what need did we have of one? It wasn't as if we had important appointments to keep. Breakfast coincided with the morning sun coming up in the east and the beginning of the work day. The sun directly above meant lunchtime, and the sun doing down in the west signified quitting time, followed by dinner. Life for us was indeed simple at the time, but unfortunately it didn't remain so.

"Stay out of trouble and stay off the farmer's property."

We heard *Mamá*, with her firm, husky voice and furrowed brow, as we fled into the beautiful, rain-drenched day. The farmer often complained to Salvador about things going missing and the marauding Mexican children he blamed for their disappearance. "They have no business on my property," he said more than a few times. According to him, there were only two places we belonged: the fields and the camp grounds. It made us smile when Salvador warned us against venturing off camp into the farmer's property. As clans living in close quarters and deplorable conditions, surrounded by what looked like opulence, we didn't see a little sharing as unreasonable. We called it sharing. The farmer called it stealing. But it wasn't as if we were asking him to share his shiny cars, beautiful boats, or the food off his fine walnut table. If a hammer, hand saw, or some lumber went missing from a shed, who was the worse for it? Not that any of this was lost on *Mamá*. She tried to keep a close eye on our shenanigans. She and the farmer could not have been more different, but they did share a common dislike for what we called "sharing."

She didn't care what we called it; if she discovered we had relieved the farmer or anyone else of something that didn't belong to us, we were dealt with quickly and severely. We may have been poor Mexican migrant workers, but we lived under an explicit code to conduct ourselves honorably at all times. I wish we could have always acted as honorably as she exhorted us to.

After breakfast, with *Mamá*'s admonition ringing in our ears, we scattered. As usual, the girls stayed behind to clean up. As I look back on those times, I cannot recall my sisters enjoying the freedoms we boys were afforded. When I look in the rearview mirror of memories, they are always beside *Mamá*, dish towel or broom in hand.

On the way out the door, I asked Juan where he was going. I loved following him around because he was always building something or doing something creative. Juan was not the kind of kid who could be idle for long. I knew he was going to be up to something interesting, and if possible—which was not always the case—I wanted to be part of it. Sometimes he was agreeable, and other times reticent. I was hoping this was going to be one of his agreeable moments.

Juan didn't acknowledge me. He walked away from the cabin with purpose, and I quietly tagged behind for a minute. I was sure he didn't know I was behind him until he suddenly stopped and turned around. I guess he decided I wasn't going away. He grabbed me gently by my bony shoulders and told me to go find some friends to play with.

"I don't have time for you or your questions today," he said, and then walked off into the woods. Undaunted, I continued to follow him, albeit at a greater distance. He must have thought it was going to be easy to get rid of me. And actually, it would have been, had he been willing to be gruff or mean, which he wasn't. When he turned, he saw me again. He paused to let me catch up, but when he stopped, I stopped too. I looked apprehensively at him across the distance between us. He looked at me and with his index finger motioned for me to come over. When I got to him, he had his hands on his hips and was shaking his head.

"Listen, Ramón. I'm going to look for a big piece of wood. That's it, nothing more." Perhaps he was hoping that would be boring enough for me to lose interest and leave him alone. Small chance of that!

"What for?" I asked excitedly. This sounded like another one of his adventures into building something cool.

"If you have to know, I want to make a baseball bat. I'm tired of playing baseball with sticks and tin cans."

Juan loved baseball, but we didn't own gloves, balls, or bats. Camp baseball was played with sticks for bats and tin cans for balls. And the tin cans were not the light aluminum pop cans you find now. They were heavy-gauge food tins. When a sharp drive was hit, it was prudent to be standing just out of the range of the swiftly moving projectile but close enough to field it quickly as it hit the ground. If you've ever been hit in the head by a fast-traveling sturdy tin can, you know what I mean. On more than one occasion, someone standing too close got nailed in the head. If the tin can caught you just right, it opened a nasty, bloody gash, and you were done for the afternoon. Although, for us, there was no such thing as going to the ER for stitches. We made do with Band-Aids and isopropyl alcohol. If there was no isopropyl alcohol, tequila could always be found.

"Where you going to find a big piece of wood? I asked.

"I'm not sure, but I saw an old barn down the road on the farmer's property a few days ago. It looks like the perfect place to explore."

"Yeah, but…" I started to object.

"Yeah, I know what you're going to say. That's why I didn't want you following me. I know you can't keep your big mouth shut and would probably tell *Mamá* I was sneaking around the farmer's property, and then I would be in trouble." I knew Juan hated being in trouble with *Mamá* more than a shot to the head from a flying tin can.

"If you let me come with you, I promise I won't say a word to anyone," I pleaded.

Juan looked around to see if anyone was watching us. He pursed his lips, rolled his eyes, and gave me a look. "Okay, fine. You already know too much. You can come, but you can't talk a lot and you have to do exactly what I tell you. I have things to do and I can't stand around in the rain answering questions and listening to you go on about heaven knows what. Do you understand?"

"Of course. I won't say a word and I'll do what you tell me," I assured him. "Boy, this is going to be fun, huh?" I said before I caught myself and zipped my mouth.

Juan paused, closed his eyes for a second, and shook his head in dismay as he turned and walked away. He was muttering to himself as I followed a couple yards behind as we left the camp grounds and entered the dark, wet woods. We walked about ten minutes on a narrow path through the steady rainfall. The thick forest and our light jean coats helped keep us from getting soaked, but we were still getting wet and cold. When I couldn't take the suspense any longer, I broke my promise.

"Where exactly is this barn, Juan?" I blurted. He looked at me sideways and laughed.

"I didn't think you could shut up for more than a couple minutes," he said and continued walking. Not getting my question answered, but unwilling to push it, I followed in silence, getting wetter and colder. After a few more minutes, the trail forked. He took the left fork, and about ten yards off the path, we encountered an old barbed wire fence. As we stood by the fence, we could see the old barn about seventy-five yards in the distance. Juan put his foot on the bottom strand and lifted the next one, making room for me to get through. He motioned for me to hurry.

"Hey, I don't know about this, Juan. You know what *Mamá* said…"

"Listen, stupid. You wanted to come with me and I told you it was okay as long as you shut your mouth and did as you were told. If you want to stand here in the rain, getting wet and cold, that's your business. I'm going to explore the barn. Oh, and I hope you can find your way back to camp," he added.

Juan new my propensity for getting lost. He always said I could get lost in the outhouse. He wasn't lying. I could walk out into the woods a hundred feet from our cabin and be totally disoriented. My sense of direction was without compass. With *Mamá*'s words echoing in my head, I stood and looked at him.

He squeezed through the parted strands of rusty barbed wire and when he got to the other side of the fence, he looked around to make sure no one was watching. Seeing no one, he ran for the barn. If possible, the rain began to fall harder. It was one of those heavy Northwest rains that often sent the Skagit River over its banks and made lakes out of pasture land. Then, in the distance, I heard the rumble of thunder, then saw the flash of lightening that followed. Not distant enough for me. As I watched Juan moving across the pasture, I wondered if the thunder and lightning were bad omens. I began to question my decision to follow Juan. The rain didn't bother me as much as the thunder and lightning. Nothing freaked me out more than lightning. No matter where I was, I was convinced it was going to hit me.

In the second I saw it, I had two choices: run for the barn, or turn around and run back to camp. Standing in the rain, waiting for the lightning to strike me was not an option. And honestly, running through the woods looking for camp didn't resonate with me either. I really only had one choice. Without further deliberation, I parted two strands of barbed wire, squeezed through, and broke into an all-out sprint across the soaked pasture.

The barn door was off its hinges, leaning awkwardly up against one side of the barn, leaving a gaping hole exposing its internals. The huge wooden barn was old, and from its dilapidated appearance I knew it had not been used for anything but storage in years. From the looks of the rough-hewn boards, the wood for the barn was probably harvested from cedar trees cleared from the property over fifty years ago. Small independently owned saw mills, used to buzz up local timber for barns and sheds, were common throughout the rural areas, but now only a few remained.

The barn had once been painted red but had long ago lost its bright color. Under the eaves where the sun or weather hadn't had access, you could still find patches of dull red, a hint of what it had been. Now, it was more bare exposed wood than paint. The wood siding was also beginning to warp under nails loosened by years of hot summers followed by cold winters and strong northern winds.

The farmer had built a smaller, more functional aluminum structure closer to his house and, for all appearances, abandoned this behemoth. It was located on the back fifty acres of the property, totally hidden from prying eyes by years of wild, untended alder saplings and blackberry bushes. How Juan found it was testament to his wandering spirit and unwillingness to listen to anyone telling him he couldn't do something.

What sun was able to penetrate the falling rain shone through the massive hole left by the missing barn door, illuminating an assortment of abandoned mounds of damp, molding hay, rusty machinery, and old and broken outdated furniture.

I caught up to Juan and raced by him into the shelter of the barn. My noisy entrance startled a handful of nesting pigeons. They frightened me as they flapped overhead, escaping out the massive hole of the missing barn door. Afraid to go in any farther, I waited for Juan.

"The thunder and lightning change your mind?" Juan smiled as he walked in after me.

"The only thing I hate more than lightning is onions," I said nervously.

"Well, onions can't kill you, but that lightning may. So, are you going to stay?" he asked, still smiling. It was a pointless question and we both knew it. Juan chuckled.

The first thing we encountered was outdated, rusty, broken-down farm machinery. There was a hay rake, some plows, and a hay baler. Next was an assortment of old furniture and a stack of wood the farmer probably planned to use but had long ago forgotten. In the back, we could see about thirty musty, deteriorating bales of hay. Some of the bales had grass growing out of them where pigeon droppings full of grass seeds had landed on them.

Juan began to rummage through the remains left to the ruin of time and weather. He finally uncovered a stack of old, dry four-by-fours and picked one out. It was about ten feet long. He found two benches and laid the four-by-four across them. He then sat next to one end, reached into his coat pocket, and pulled out a knife I'd never seen before. The knife had an eight-inch rusty brown blade with a wooden handle. To be safe, you could fold the blade into the handle.

Juan removed a sharpening file from the same pocket and began to work the blade. I wondered where he got the knife and file but didn't want to chance having to find my way back to the camp alone. Although I knew deep down he would never abandon me in the woods, I played along at being afraid he would. I sat and watched him sharpen the blade. He worked at it until he turned the dull, rusty blade into a sharp, bright, silvery piece of metal. When he felt it was sharp enough, he started whittling on the bone-dry four-by-four. It was slow work, but Juan was patient, strong, and methodical. I was used to sitting and watching him make things.

"Are you making a bat?" I said.

"Yes, that's what I told you I was going to make."

"That's a big piece of wood. It's going to take you a long time."

"I'm going to work on it until it's finished, and you can't say anything to anyone."

"Where did you get the knife and that thing you used to sharpen it? I was finally willing to ask.

"I found it in one of the farmer's sheds."

"One of the sheds on the farmer's property you were not supposed to be in?" I smiled.

"Do you think you can find your way back to camp on your own?" He chuckled.

"What do you think *Mamá* is going to say when she sees the knife?"

"She's never going to know I have it, because she's never going to see it. Do you understand?" He took a moment to give me a stern look.

"Yes. I understand."

"Good. Now, while I work on this piece of wood, I want you to explore the rest of the barn and see if you can find a hand saw," he said, whittling away.

"Sounds good," I said. "That's a job I like. Exploring things."

Juan whittled on the four-by-four for a few hours. The wood was soft and fairly easy to sculpt. When his hands got sore, he stopped and rested. After a few minutes of rubbing the soreness out of his hands, he continued.

As I explored, I found broken wooden chairs and tables, worn-out, stained mattresses, and doors with metal hinges still attached. I sat in the seat on the hay rake for a while, manipulating the up-down lever, pretending it was a floor shifter on a hot rod. I climbed on the hay baler that was sitting up against the ladder leading to the upper floor. From the second floor, I could see the tops of the alder saplings and, in the distance, acres and acres of pine trees. For a long while, I sat with my feet dangling out the open second-story door, watching the rain form pools of water between the trees. The dark clouds were moving north and away from us. It seemed like the rain was moving with the clouds and no longer falling as heavy. I figured we'd been in the barn a good four hours when the heavy rain turned to a light drizzle. Juan called for me to come down. He had stopped whittling. He said his hands were sore and he had a blister in the palm of his right hand where he'd held the knife.

"Did you find a saw?" he asked.

"Oops, I forgot I was looking for one."

"You're a Knucklehead Fred," he said, shaking his head.

"What's a Knucklehead Fred?"

"Never mind."

"I did find a big, heavy box by the rake, but I couldn't open it."

When Juan was able to pry the lid off the wooden box, we found it heavy with farm machinery tools, none of which was any use to us. Juan closed the box and walked to the opening where the barn door once hung. He stood looking at his blister.

"Maybe you should have looked for some gloves in the farmer's shed."

"Humm…good idea. Well, we better get back to camp." He picked up the four-by-four and hid it behind the hay. He left the knife and sharpening file in a drawer of an old dresser. The sun was streaking through low-moving clouds in a bright blue sky as we walked quietly back to camp. When we neared the camp, he stopped and turned to face me.

"Are you going to keep your mouth shut?"

"About what?" I inquired, throwing my hands in the air, feigning ignorance.

"Good," he said, and smiled.

I kept my promise and said nothing to anyone about our foray onto the farmer's property. Juan's secrecy didn't so much have to do with not wanting anyone to know he was making a bat as it did with being on the farmer's property, in his barn, abandoned or not. That information could get us thrown out of camp at a time when we needed the money to survive.

So every day after work, Juan and I took our showers, ate dinner, and together, sneaked out of camp, into the woods, and out to the barn. Each day, without a word, I fell in behind him. When he got to the fence, he put his foot on the bottom wire and grabbed the next one and pulled them apart. He turned and motioned for me to go through. When we got to the barn, the wood sharpening file and knife were always where he had left them. On Thursday afternoon, before he started to work on sharpening the knife blade, he pulled out a pair of gloves.

"Where did you find them?" I asked.

"Same place I found the other stuff. I couldn't find leather gloves, just these cloth ones. They'll have to do."

He sharpened the knife again and continued whittling. I sat quietly and watched. I don't know what it was about watching him work that kept my attention. Sometimes he sang or whistled quietly to himself as he worked. Sometimes he talked to himself.

On Wednesday of the following week, the four-by-four was finally looking like a crude bat. Juan was giving the old piece of wood a second life. As he worked, he muttered to himself about what or how he was doing. He expertly took a little off here and a little bit there.

Off and on, he worked on the bat for ten days. When Juan finally quit, it was a warm sunny day, edging toward the cool of the coming evening. The sun was a blood orange in the distant horizon when Juan began putting things away. I had been upstairs rummaging around when I found what he'd sent me looking for on the first day. I came down the stairs and handed the saw to him. He smiled.

"Is this what you were looking for?" I asked.

"Yeah, it's rusty, but I think it will still cut," he said. As I sat on the four-by-four to hold it steady, he sawed off approximately four feet from the end he'd been whittling on. That made it easier to refine what he'd already shaped with the knife. He then rolled it on the barn floor to check symmetry and balance and was surprised to find he'd done a good job with the tools he had.

When he'd hidden the wood, file, gloves, and knife, we walked back into the woods and made our way back to the camp.

"How long do you think it's going to take you to finish the bat?" I asked.

"I think by Sunday, maybe."

"Maybe we can use it in one of our games soon."

"Well, we still need a ball. I'm tired of using a tin can. It's a poor excuse for a ball."

"Where do you think you can get a ball?" I asked.

"I'm not sure, but I'm working on that too."

He had his hands deep in his front pockets as he walked through the woods. I put my hands in my front pockets too. I tried to walk like him but my short legs weren't as efficient or as long and I had to skip a few steps to keep up.

One day as he was whittling, I asked Juan where he got the idea of making a bat. He told me when we were working the strawberry field closest to the farmer's home a few weeks ago, he had seen the farmer's children playing baseball. He thought, watching them, that if he could find the right piece of wood and a knife to carve with, he could make a bat and even a mitt, if he could find some leather. He wasn't sure about a ball. He said he first wanted to work on the bat because he felt it was going to be the easiest. When he got the bat finished, he would work on the mitt and then try to figure out how to get a good ball.

It was rare that there was a Saturday that we didn't have to be in the fields. After breakfast, *Mamá* dispatched Juan and Enrique to cut enough wood to last through the following week. Since I'd split the bottom of my boot with the axe while chopping wood early in the summer, I had not been allowed to handle an axe. Not that I minded. I had been lucky I hadn't chopped my foot in two. After they had replenished the wood supply, Juan and I disappeared back into the woods. His project was close to completion. When we got to the barn, he pulled the almost finished bat from behind a bale of hay. He'd been working on it every spare minute away from the fields, and it finally looked like the real thing. After whittling on it for a while, he stopped and pulled out a couple pieces of rough, rust-colored paper.

"What is that?" I asked him.

"It's called sandpaper. It's used on a rough piece of wood so it looks and feels smooth. Here, feel how rough it is?" He handed me a piece. It felt harsh.

"I guess I don't need to ask where you got the sandpaper," I said. A slight smile came across his lips, but he didn't say anything. I knew the answer before I made the comment, but made it anyway.

He held the handle end of the bat with his left hand and placed the thick end on the barn floor and began to rub the sandpaper up and down the bat from top to bottom while turning it round and round. After about thirty minutes of sanding, he stopped and ran his hand over the length of the bat and nodded affirmatively to himself. He got to his feet, took a hitter's stance, and took a few swings in the air. It was bigger than the one he'd seen the farmer's kid use, but he'd purposefully made it that way. He wanted it to be better as well, but that was yet to be seen.

"Is it finished?" I asked.

"Pretty much, but I want to do one last thing," he said, and then sat down and began to carve something into the bat. I watched. When he finished, I could read the word Slugger in large letters across the bat.

"Now is it finished?" I asked.

"Nope. One more thing. Didn't you find a cast-iron pan the other day?" he asked.

"Yeah, what about it?"

"Go get it."

I returned a moment later with a black cast-iron pan and handed it to him. He gathered up some wood shavings, put them in the pan, and walked into the clearing about ten feet from the barn. He pulled out a handful of matches, gathered the shavings into a small pile, and set them alight. He blew on them to make them burn hotter and brighter. After burning the shavings down to a small pile of ashes, he walked back into the barn and sat down.

"What was that all about?" I asked.

"You'll see. I have to let the ashes cool for a few minutes."

When they were cool enough, he put some of the ashes

into the palm of his hand and spit on them. He then began to rub the ashes into the word Slugger, until the word stood out black in contrast to the light wood. When he was done, he held it up for me to see.

"Wow!" I said. "It really looks cool now."

"Yes, it does, but now we need a ball," he said. I have to think about it. I also have to find some leather to make some gloves."

"Where are we going to find some leather?" I asked, as he put the gloves, knife, sharpening file, and sandpaper into the dresser drawer.

"Don't really know," he confessed, as we headed across the field toward the fence. "I'm hoping the farmer has some laying around in one of his sheds and he'll let me borrow some." Although I couldn't see his face, I was sure he was smiling when he said borrow.

As I followed Juan back to the camp, I told him I was glad he never left me in the woods because I was sure I could never have found my way back to camp. He just laughed.

"If you get lost out here, there is only one thing you need to remember to find your way back. Look: Right now, where is the sun?"

"Over there." I pointed west.

"That direction is west. The sun always sets in the west. That is the direction the camp is in. So, we follow the sun back to camp. In the morning when we get up, you notice that the sun is rising, don't you? That direction is east. To get to the barn, you walk east, in the direction of the rising sun. Remember, the sun rises in the east and sets in the west."

"Okay," I said. "But I know there is an easier way."

"Yeah, I know you do. Following me, right?"

"Yeah, I won't get lost following you."

I couldn't see his face, but I knew he was smiling again. He always smiled. That was just Juan.

Juan didn't show the finished bat to anyone right then. There would be too many question he didn't want to answer. He went straight into our cabin and placed it on the ledge above the door where no one would see it. When I asked him when we were going to use it, he said he wanted to wait until he could find a ball. Hitting tin cans with it would ruin it. The knife, sharpening file, sandpaper, and gloves became part of our hidden stash to be used for future projects. We never revealed our elicit forays onto the farmer's property to anyone. If *Mamá*, the farmer, or Salvador ever found out, I never heard about it.

Salvador did mention some items missing from one of the farmer's sheds, but of course, we knew nothing about that!

I—NOT AS GOOD, SAYS WHO?

I—Not As Good, Says Who?

I—not as good, say you, and why?
Twice down the clothes I wear and worn?
Confused, to look at you and see the hate, I sigh.

Spick! You spit and vomit scorn!
Innocent I am, young, alone, afraid, without a say,
No less, are made to reassess my blood and wonder
born.

What validation I ask, have you to show and make
you say,
As only time and fate, the difference show,
That makes you part of all and I, forlorn, a stray?

Conspicuously poor, to walk in fields of dust that
blow,
Against earth's inanimates transgress, labor, and
contend.
But still your insults add to injury with frigid hearts
of stone.

Silent—you wish invisible…lives worthy to defend,
Against Pharisees in child's pants who mock and
seek appeal,
With blameless tongue to Pilate—hands washed,
willing to pretend,

That they and you are guileless, so little left to feel,
For sins against unfortunates and ones untouched of
destiny.
For martyr, holy I refuse to veil, not adequate to seal,

By heaven's fate—yet lies before me, in tragic infamy,
While still plot I, your fall—those haughty eyes from
virtuous perch,
You hide behind self-righteousness to plot demise—
calamity.

Innocent—once, child I was, for wiser now I search,
To exorcise my demons, their legion I've disguised,
As darkness falls, it's you they seek, and live for your
demise.

I—not as good, you say, and why?

I—NOT AS GOOD, SAYS WHO?

Beautiful Like You

When the worn brakes squealed
And we came to a stop,
Currents of swirling dust
Caught up to us:
Engulfed us,
As we sat with our eyes closed
And mouths covered,
On the back of the two-ton
Flatbed Chevy truck.

When the dust passed
And our vision cleared,
We could breathe again.
We stood on wobbly legs,
Tired from five hours
On the road
As *Mamá* dusted us off.
It was then we saw
Where we were…

Four rows of five
Stood in the cool of a waning,
Scorching summer day.
Ancient structures:
Windowless, wooden shacks,
Weary from their burden
Disgracefully sat,
Inhabited by dust-choked,
Sun-baked Mexicans…brown,
In threadbare cotton T-shirts
And patched and faded Wrangler jeans.

The smell of boiling
Pinto beans and thick corn tortillas
Wafted in the humid air
Over the chatter of dark-haired,
Wide-eyed children playing in the dirt.
As we disembarked,
They stopped playing and stared.
"Why are we stopping here, *Mamá*?" I asked.
"This is where we're going to stay, *M'ijo*.
This is where the work is."

BEAUTIFUL LIKE YOU

As we carried our blankets, pillows,
And extra clothes in our arms,
Salvador, the camp foreman, pointed us toward
The last two cabins in row three.
One for the boys and the other for the girls.

Young boys carried fire wood
Into cabins as serious mothers stirred
Black cast-iron skillets filled with rice.
The familiar scent of cumin,
Chili powder, and garlic
Filled our nostrils as we walked by.

Old men sat on wooden benches
Smoking—playing cards
And drinking Olympia beer
On wooded picnic tables.
They nodded respectfully as we walked by.

When we reached our cabins
I tugged at *Mamá*'s sleeve.
"We can't be happy here, *Mamá*.
We don't know anyone
And look how dirty it is," I said.

BEAUTIFUL LIKE YOU

"*Si, M'ijo*, it is dirty, but we will clean it up
And look at all the children.
You will make new friends
And as long as we are together,
We will always be happy."
"But it is so ugly, *Mamá*," I pleaded.
"*Si, M'ijo*, but I will plant pretty flowers
All around us soon.
Everywhere, it will be a garden of beautiful colors."
"*Si, Mamá*, it will be beautiful—"

Beautiful like you.

The Wrestling Match

The migrant shacks we lived in were back a ways, well hidden from the main road that led into Sedro-Woolley, a small logging community in Western Washington. A person traveling on State Highway 20 saw nothing but beautiful, tall, fifty-year-old cedars lining the north side of the road. Like most of Washington's natural forests, the area had been extensively logged in the early part of the century, but was growing back well. Blanketing the cedar trunks was a thick, dense layer of blackberry bushes. They climbed the lower branches and hung heavy with lush, black, seedy fruit. Their needle-sharp thorns made them impenetrable by anything but rabbits and field mice.

It was the perfect facade to hide a labor camp behind—a camp nobody wanted to see or even admit existed. Out of sight, out of mind, as they say. We were the ghosts living in a place that didn't exist. And we didn't enjoy living there any more than the community enjoyed having us there.

Some of the strawberry fields we worked were located close to the camp; others were scattered all over Skagit County. Strawberries were a cash crop and big Northwest business. The twenty-five-acre field we had been working that week was a hundred yards back from the farmer's house. To get to it, we walked a rough, circuitous gravel road through densely forested acreage. About halfway between the field and the camp was the farmer's house. The road ran alongside the house for a short distance before emptying onto Highway 20, which then wound up into the North Cascades and on to Eastern Washington. On our way between the fields and the camp, at one point, the road was close enough to the house you could easily hit it with a stone.

This was a difficult path for me, because it was summer. When the weather turned warm, often the farmer's children could be heard and seen playing in what seemed like a paradise of lush green yard. They had a swimming pool, a swing set, croquet, baseball bats, gloves and balls, basketballs, and heaven knows what else. And yes, I begrudged them their wealth, their toys, and all the free time to play away the summer. A short distance away, we labored in the dirt and hot sun from sunup to sundown. In my child's mind, it didn't seem right. In my child's mind, all children should have at least some of what they had—and none of what we were experiencing.

As a child, I only understood what hurt. From what we could see on our frequent walks around their house, the farmer's family consisted of two daughters and a son. One daughter was about seven, the other maybe thirteen. We'd seen the boy driving a pickup around the farm so we assumed he was about fifteen or sixteen.

If *Mamá* was with us as we walked along the driveway, she would exhort us not to stare. She thought it impolite. *Mamá* placed great emphasis on being respectful, discreet, and polite. And she knew from experience that too much staring could cause conflict. Someone occasionally took offense and that was when trouble started. The farmer's children would complain to their mother. Then at dinner, she would discuss with their father what was to be done about those prying eyes. The farmer invariable spoke to Salvador, the camp foreman, who went from shack to shack, warning us to stay away from the farmer's property and children. Not that they ever had reason to complain specifically about our family's behavior.

Mamá had trained us well in the etiquette of being poor browns around the rich whites: divert your eyes; don't talk to them unless asked; and, first and foremost, keep your distance. In many ways we understood what life was like in the South for blacks. We lived under mostly unspoken, yet very clear, social restrictions.

Mamá also knew how much emotional pain it caused us. To divert our attention, she sometimes talked to us softly as we walked past. *Mamá* has a naturally soothing voice and it worked wonders to calm her inquisitive boys. The situation must have pained her; she desperately wanted something better for us. Knowing something better wasn't possible now, but understanding that it was waiting somewhere in our future, she took to reassuring us with her visions. Often, her hypnotic, soft Spanish voice carried us past the house with the massive, perfectly manicured lawn without emotional incident. On the occasions she went before us and we followed later, we, of course, walked more slowly, stared discreetly, and felt sick with envy. On our own, mostly out of youthful ignorance and curiosity, we put ourselves in harm's way. But with her, we were always safe.

On one particular day, we were on our own. It was Juan, Enrique, Mario, and I making our way home from the fields. *Mamá*, Raquel, Dolores, and Linda had left the fields about thirty minutes before us to start dinner and have it waiting for us. We were left to check in our flats of strawberries and follow. *Mamá* often did that, because it was understood it was harder to get into mischief with a belly full of beans and that keeping us fed was as good as nourishing our minds with dreams.

As we boys passed the farmer's house, we noticed the

children playing on the lawn. The boy looked like he was trying to coax his thirteen-year-old sister into wrestling with him on the lawn. He wore what we thought was a rather immodest-looking, tight-fitting nylon uniform we had never seen before. Enrique chuckled and asked Juan what the hell the kid was wearing. Juan just shook his head and smiled.

"I have no idea, but I wouldn't be caught alive or dead wearing it in camp. People might get the wrong impression about me." He laughed and kept moving along the gravel drive, still watching the play on the lawn, but not in an obvious manner.

The boy grabbed his sister's arm, pulled her toward him, went to one knee, and lifted her onto his shoulders. He then began to twirl her around while she screamed bloody murder. While he carried her around the yard, she screamed for him to put her down. Her screams didn't sound excited or playful. There certainly didn't appear to be any love lost between them. We stopped and stood, gawking for a moment, wondering where this was going, and if we might need to intervene. Hearing *Mamá*'s admonitions playing in my ear, I knew we shouldn't have stopped, but there we stood, nevertheless. It might have had the potential for a bad outcome. Then again, it could have just been fun and games between older brother and younger sister. After a few too many twirls, as evidenced by her continued screaming, her brother put her down roughly. He was laughing. She was cursing and unable to walk straight. She looked sick and walked like she was drunk. The boy noticed us watching him.

"For your information, that was a wrestling move called the fireman's carry," he informed us. "Do you guys know anything about wrestling?"

"No," Juan told him. "But it doesn't look very difficult, especially when you are wrestling your sister. How hard could it be?"

The boy bristled at Juan's implication that he might not be that tough or just wrestled girls.

"I was just playing with my sister," he spat. "I'm on the varsity wrestling team at Sedro-Woolley High School and will probably go to state this year." We had no idea what state he was talking about but felt comfortable with him leaving this one if he wanted.

"Do you have to wear that funny suit when you wrestle?" Enrique inquired. The boy puffed out his chest. "It's the wrestling uniform all high school wrestlers wear. Do you guys want to come over and wrestle me?" he asked.

"All of us?" inquired Enrique.

"I'll take you one at a time. Who wants to be first?" he asked, confidently getting down in a funny looking stance. I did some quick calculations. If he was in high school, it meant he was at least a couple years older than Juan and maybe three years older than Enrique. Not that the boy's age mattered to Enrique. He was always game for a fight. He leaned forward to accept the challenge and be the first one, but Juan grabbed his arm and pulled him back. Being oldest, if anyone was going to accept the challenge to wrestle or fight, it was going to be him. I think he was also being protective. Since *Mamá* and *Papá* had split and our older brothers were gone, even at his young age, Juan readily accepted the role of protector.

He might have only been fourteen, but that made him the oldest male and, therefore, in charge when *Mamá* wasn't around. He took his role seriously, and it couldn't have fallen on stronger, more competent shoulders. Not that Enrique would not have made a worthy opponent, state wrestler or not. Enrique was not the kind to back down from any kind of fight, unless it was against Juan. Enrique knew his limits and Juan's potential. We had all seen Juan fight in camp boxing matches and usually against adult men who thought it would be fun to beat up on a kid, only to find themselves returning to their shacks with black eyes, split lips, and bloody noses.

The boy was clearly taller and heavier than any of us. To me, he looked like a pretty rough customer, but then most did. I was what you might call a wimp, inside and out. The only fighting I did was holding back tears. They called me *el llorón*, the crier, because when my feelings were hurt, which was way too often, I readily cried. And fighting of any kind was not my game.

"I'll wrestle you," Juan said confidently.

"Have you ever wrestled before?" the boy asked.

"No, but how hard can it be?" Juan smiled.

"Harder than you think. I've wrestled for years. It takes a lot of training and you have to be tough. Since you've never wrestled before, I'll take it easy on you," the boy said, motioning Juan to come into the yard to engage him.

As a rule, playing with Mexicans was not something white kids did. But his father was probably somewhere on a tractor, and his mother, busy doing her nails and sipping an afternoon gin and tonic. Neither would be the wiser.

Since he had his wrestling uniform on, I felt he really wanted to show off. He could not resist the opportunity to put some Mexican kids in their place. So, he crouched down again into what I would later learn was a typical wrestling stance and began to circle Juan, counterclockwise. I could see Juan wasn't entirely sure what to make of him. I'm sure he was at least slightly reluctant to wrestle a boy in a girly-looking outfit. Juan glanced back momentarily with a quizzical look on his face. Enrique elbowed me.

"This is going to be good," Enrique said, smiling.

The boy lunged at Juan. Being overly confident, he overcommitted himself, and Juan, being whippet quick, easily sidestepped him. The boy landed on his hands and knees in the grass beside Juan. He got up quickly, jerked around, and came at Juan again. In earnest and with renewed resolve, he began to circle Juan. Juan planted his feet, bent slightly at the knees, and leaned forward. The boy feigned a lunge a couple times, hoping to throw Juan off balance, but Juan didn't react. When he thought Juan wasn't expecting him, he attacked again. This time, Juan slapped him aside. The head slap was painfully audible to us all. The boy landed on his hands and knees again. I remember thinking, "Oh shit. Now Juan's really pissed him off."

When he got to his feet, the boy's face was flushed enough that you couldn't tell where Juan had slapped him. His eyes had narrowed. He reached up and touched the side of his face where Juan had landed the sharp, solid slap.

"You fucking chickenshit spick, you going to wrestle me or not?"

Enrique and I looked at each other. Suddenly, the air around us felt dangerous. I had a queasy feeling in my gut and I wanted us to leave. Now!

I thought, "Oh shit, now he put his foot in it."

Juan's body stiffened visibly at the taunt. Although we were bronzed brown from our labor in the sun, I could still see the back of Juan's neck and ears flash crimson. I wanted to say something, anything, to get Juan to just back away, but my fear was paralyzing. I would've thrown up if I opened my mouth. I've always had this reaction to violence. I looked at Enrique. He was grinning. I just stood and waited. "Oh, God, I think we should leave," I whispered.

"I don't think he should have called Juan that. Now it's going to get ugly," Enrique said.

"Maybe I didn't hear you right. What did you call me?" Juan asked, cocking his head slightly to the left, like a bird does when it wants to get a better look at you. Juan avoided fights outside camp whenever possible, and I could tell he wanted to give the boy a way out of what had quickly turned into a potentially serious situation. The boy would have none of it.

"I called you a fucking chickenshit spick. Are you afraid I'm going to kick your ass, spick?" he snarled, spittle spraying from his mouth. His fists were clenched and he was shaking.

"That's what I thought you said. Okay, if that's what you want, let's wrestle," Juan said in a serious tone he rarely used. I knew it to mean it was too late for praying.

The boy once again got down in his wrestler's stance and now more recklessly began to circle Juan. Juan watched him carefully. When he lunged, Juan sidestepped him again. The boy fell hard. He got up and just as he was turning, Juan was already in midair. At the exact moment the boy squared, Juan drove his shoulder into the boy's chest and knocked him off his feet. The force of the blow sent them a good distance from the point of impact. When they hit the ground—hard—Juan landed on top. You could hear the air whoosh out of the boy's lungs, like a balloon deflating. Not knowing proper wrestling protocol, instead of pinning him, Juan sat on his stomach, straddling him.

The boy struggled to get up and catch his breath, but Juan had his right hand around his throat. After some ineffectual thrashing around, he finally screamed for Juan to get off him. Juan relented, stood up quickly, and readied himself for the next assault. The boy rolled onto his hands and knees, wheezing and coughing, struggling to get his breath back. Juan waited patiently. When the boy regained his breath, he yelled at Juan.

"This time, I'm not going to be so nice. I'm going to really kick your fucking ass."

Without warning, he lunged at Juan. Juan didn't move an inch. When the boy got within range, Juan brought his right foot up and kicked him in the balls. In that one short, swift movement, he focused all the pain and anger the taunts had engendered in all of us.

The boy dropped to the ground and began to vomit. We held our breath as he writhed in agonizing pain. All the color drained from his pale skin; he looked ashen. Without a word, knowing the wrestling match was over Juan turned and walked away. As he left the yard, he picked up a baseball he saw lying nearby and flicked it to Enrique. Cobra quick, Enrique snatched the ball out of the air and put it in his pocket.

"I think kicking him in the balls might have been an illegal wrestling move," Enrique said, laughing, as we walked quickly away.

"He shouldn't have called me that. I hate that name."

As we walked away, we heard the boy's sister, who had been watching the entire match, yelling at him. "Maybe if you trained harder and didn't walk around the house in my underwear and bra when Mom and Dad are at church, you wouldn't have gotten your ass kicked by that wimpy Mexican."

Surprised by what she said, we turned to look as she ran into the house.

"Let that be a lesson to you, boys. Tough guys don't wear their sister's underwear!" Juan exclaimed as we hurried along the road.

"And I don't think they wear shiny, girly tights either," Enrique added.

"Boy, when *Mamá* finds out what you did, we're all going to get a whipping," I said.

"Oh, shut up!" responded Enrique. Juan was silent but he knew it was the truth. There was nothing he hated more than being in trouble with *Mamá*. He expected better of himself. He knew she expected better of him too. His silence spoke volumes about how he regretted what had happened.

We ate dinner with downcast eyes in silence. *Mamá* knew there was something wrong. Her intuition was darn right spooky sometimes.

"*¿Qué pasó?*" she said, scanning our faces. Knowing trouble would ensue, any one of us would have lied to her, but that wasn't Juan's way. Regardless of the consequences, Juan always told the truth.

He stopped eating. With tears welling up in his eyes, he told her the whole story. When he finished, *Mamá* stood with her arms crossed over her chest and her mouth agape. She shook her head and warned us Salvador would probably be paying us a visit soon. She scolded us for a couple minutes, but it was more fear than anger at Juan. The work was important and the last thing we needed was to be kicked out of camp. I could tell she wasn't really upset at us. As she turned to fetch a tortilla off the woodstove, I could see her eyes cloud up from worry. And, I'm sure it was more than the loss of work that caused her great concern. She was probably afraid Juan might be arrested. She picked a couple tortillas off the stove and gently placed them on the table in front of us and said nothing more.

After dinner she took us to see Salvador. She asked Juan to tell him the story. As he did so, Salvador smiled ever so slightly. He didn't want us to get the impression he condoned what Juan had done, but couldn't help himself. Although he never said, I doubted he cared for the farmer any more than we did. When Juan finished, Salvador looked puzzled.

"That boy had to be at least two or three years older than you, Juan. And you kicked him in the balls?" he said, incredulously.

"Yes, but only after he called me a spick and some other stuff," Juan explained.

"What other stuff?" asked Salvador.

"Stuff I can't repeat. We don't say words like that," he responded, looking at *Mamá*. I could tell she was proud of Juan's response.

"Okay. Thank you," he said, and excused us.

We walked away but *Mamá* stayed behind to chat with him. She returned about thirty minutes later but never mentioned it again.

The strange thing was, we never heard a word out of the farmer either. As we talked about it in our cabin over the following week, our consensus was that neither the boy nor his sister said anything to their parents. We guessed the boy was afraid that if he said anything, his sister would tell them about her big, tough brother wearing her underwear and bra around the house. I doubted that revelation would have gone down well at dinnertime. It was probably going to remain a secret neither would ever share.

Mamá cautioned us against saying anything around camp, but our silence was not enough to keep the secret. Salvador loved gossip, and this was too good to keep to himself. It wasn't more than a few days after our meeting with him that the boys and men in camp took to calling Juan the "camp wrestling champ." The girls giggled anytime Juan was around. Once she figured we were out of trouble, *Mamá* smiled, ever so slightly, when Juan was chided by the men and boys.

But that didn't mean she didn't do something to prevent that kind of thing from ever happening again. It was the last time she permitted us to walk by the farmer's house without being present.

And that was how Juan got us a baseball. That Saturday, Juan got Slugger down for the first time and introduced it to the other boys in the camp. We still didn't have gloves, but no one complained. Slugger was too big for me and I never got the privilege of swinging the bat Juan had made by hand with such arduous labor. I did get the pleasure of hearing the Crack! when the bat made contact with the ball. Enrique and Juan both told me it felt great.

We played baseball every afternoon after work and on our days off, long into the hot summer until one evening when Juan was at bat. Because I was small and fast, they usually positioned me in center field, on the ragged edge between the pasture and where the cedar trees started. When the ball was hit hard—into the trees—I was there to track, find, and retrieve it, which I did repeatedly.

Juan swung. I heard the familiar Crack! of the bat, and watched the ball sail far over my head. As soon as I saw it flying high above me, knowing it was going deep into the woods, I ran for the darkness.

I heard it hit some branches overhead before I lost it to the muffling denseness of the trees. I stopped. Maybe I could pinpoint its position if I heard it falling through the branches or hitting the ground. Nothing. It probably landed in some soft undergrowth. I looked for a while, then walked out of the woods and summoned the gang. Everyone scoured the area for an hour and found nothing but pine cones. It was lost somewhere in the underbrush.

Off and on over the next few days, we spent more time looking, with no luck. Not long after, we moved back to Eastern Washington. I don't recall what happened to Slugger. Possibly we lost it on our move out of camp, or someone borrowed it. Maybe it was the farmer.

Hello, *Mamá*

How are you?
Can you hear me?
It's Ramón.
I know…
I know…
I haven't visited for a while.
I haven't called either.
I'm sorry, *Mamá*.
It's not that I've forgotten you…
I haven't.
How could I?

I haven't forgotten,
It was you who held me—in your arms,
When I was born,
And suckled me to your breast
And gave me life.

I haven't forgotten,
It was you who got little sleep
Those few months:
Holding, feeding, and
Keeping me safe,
All the while caring for
My brothers and sisters
While cooking and working
In the fields.

HELLO, MAMA

I haven't forgotten,
It was you who caught me—when I fell.
When I was learning to walk.

I haven't forgotten,
It was you who carried me
To the hospital
When I fell and cut
My leg.
I almost bled to death.

I haven't forgotten,
It was you who protected me,
Stood between me
And the harshness—that was my father:
Physical and emotional.
I was never very strong.

I haven't forgotten,
It was you who nursed me—day and night,
When I was sick with the flu.
I gave it to you too, didn't I?

I haven't forgotten,
It was you who washed my clothes,
And made my food—every day.
And not once did I ever
Hear you complain.
Not once did I say thank you.

HELLO, MAMA

I haven't forgotten,
It was you who sat on the wood bench,
Looking into your folded hands,
Not wanting me to see the tears
As they ran down your face
And soaked your dress
When the Greyhound bus
Took me away—to war.
And I remember it was you
Who hugged me so hard
When I returned safe,
I could barely breathe.
And it was you who
Stood so long
Outside my door.
Listening to me breathe
While I slept,
My first night home.
You didn't know,
I was watching you too,
So thankful to be home.

I haven't forgotten,
It was you who first held my children
When they were born.
I couldn't hold them because
They were so small,
I thought I would hurt them.

HELLO, MAMÁ

They're all gone now—*Mamá.*
I miss them so.
Forgive me, *Mamá,*
I'll come see you soon.
I'll hold your veined, arthritic hands,
Touch your face,
And kiss your wrinkled brow,
And tell you—in person
How much I appreciated you then:
How much I love you now.

"It's okay, M'ijo,
I know you're a busy man.
I can wait,
But not too long."

Hello, *Mamá.*

The Soil—Part 1

Pots of Soil

As an adult I spent my days in an office,
Listening to the ticking clock.
I watched with dispassionate eyes
The second hand move
Gracefully around the numbers,
As I calmly breathed to a
Count of three,
Held it for two,
Then let it go…
Forcing it silently
Into the middle of the room.

Clients came on the hour
And departed the same,
Taking with them another hour,
While the sweeping hands,
Without judgment or notice,
Moved silently around.
My office is not far from the soil and the farms
That nurtured me:
Sustained me as a child.
And, like my life on the soil,
Papá has been gone a number of years.
And although I didn't know it then,
As a child will often not,

But understand and acknowledge now—
First came the soil
And *Papá* followed thereafter.
And he was the connection to it all:
The soil and everything that followed.

He stood confidently on the soil
As he now lays serenely below it:
Like a lone wolf inhabiting the night
Or a hawk the sky,
With the confidence that it is home.

As a farmer, he owned the soil,
As much as it owned him:
He held the soil,
As much as it held him.
It was thus,
In countless ways
Even he, I'm sure, did not understand,
But accepted like I accept the rain
That gently falls on the pasture
And woods that make up my life.

Pots of soil.

La Ventana

I'm on the fifth floor
Of an office building,
Overlooking a wet, blustery park
And watching the rain speckle the windows
On a cool, fall
Seattle afternoon.

Then again—suddenly,
Without warning...

I'm lying on a bed in a migrant labor camp
Somewhere in the fertile
Willamette Valley in Oregon.
I'm listening to the music
Of the rain
As it rivets the corrugated tin roof
Above my head.
A sound I grew to love
And hate simultaneously.
Love because it kept
Us from the fields,
And hate because the drenching
Sound represented the poverty
That was my youth.
And still the contrasting feelings
Of the sounds

LA VENTANA

Live in places too sad to visit,
Yet can't escape.
I try to hide, but they find me—the memories.
They have a life of their own,
And come and go without permission.
And sometimes while I sleep,
Lying quietly in my bed,
I dream the watery windows
Are laments of my past.

I'm eating my lunch: a tuna fish sandwich
From a brown paper bag,
And looking out a window
Overlooking Lake Washington.
I see flowerbeds and green manicured lawns.
Flowers, bright and beautiful,
And lush pastoral lawns
Reflect time and space
That is my present.

Then again—suddenly,
Without warning…

It was a long, blistering, hot day
Under a torturing sun.
I'm resting in my bunk:
The time between the labor
And the meal…
When the scents of
Boiling pinto beans, cumin,

LA VENTANA

Chili powder, and onions
Waft in from the shack next door,
Mamá's cooking.
It's almost time for dinner.
The wonderful scents linger in my brain.
But they're not alone—
With them come the painful images
Of disenfranchisement and disillusionment:
A life lived on the peripheral edge
Of an unforgiving, white society
That wants to send me back
To the place of my *padres,*
A land I've never been to.
A land I have never seen.

I watch the people moving
Like ants below me.
Bright-colored maple leaves are dropping,
Riding the cold, swirling wind currents
Like happy children on a merry-go-round.

Then again, suddenly,
And without warning...

It's a balmy summer evening.
I'm standing in Pioneer Park
At the annual Sunnyside Cherry Blossom Festival.
I'm eating a hot dog...
Mustard with sweet relish.
The bright florescent flood lamps

LA VENTANA

Light up the dark,
And the sounds of screaming children
Echo and reverberate off
The brick buildings
That surround the park.

I'm watching my brothers and sisters
Ride the roller coaster:
Round and round,
Up and down.
But I'm not with them.
The fast up-and-down
Motion makes me sick.

Two worlds overlapping.
They both remain
In serenity and pain.

La ventana.

It's the Sun

For Oso Negro

It's the sun you want to feel—
Isn't it?
On your face,
Sinking deep,
Penetrating into your brown soul,
As you lie contemplatively on the deck,
Chain-smoking cigarette after cigarette
While the aromatic scents,
The fragrances of life,
Like flowers in the garden,
Are carried in the breeze
All around you.

The pasture—it's ready for mowing.
But the wind
Silently calls,
Telling you,
It's too late for sowing.

You feel your body warmed
As the smoke dissipates
And the sun penetrates,
Your marrow.

And still—
Life has been
Rutted, uphill roads.
And darkness cold
Has made you shiver,
Like the fragile
And the old,
Who will never be consoled.

There's Dylan
On the stereo,
Tequila surges through your veins
While a blackened tar eats your lungs
As you contemplate travels—past,
Anticipating travails—ahead.

Will the end come quickly?
Will you serenely wane?
What will be your last refrain?
In the end
It's all the same.
It's not the acclaim
Or what is gained.
But, how you saw the game.

IT'S THE SUN

What was it all about—
For you?
Was it family and friends?
Lovers in the end
Who came and went?
In your self-imposed solitude,
Do you lament?

When prayers turn into riches
And wishes are bridges
To more tranquil times
With Dylanesque rhymes,
Will Oso Negro feast on milk and honey?
Will *amour* cover him?
Like the multitude of flowers
On the mountainsides,
And the beautiful places
You loved to wander,
But now just in your brain
As you ponder
If you are sane.

And when Jesus comes,
As He surely will,
Want Him too or not.
You must know,
He's not just for show.

IT'S THE SUN

Even the mountains
And the lilies there,
The rocks, the trees,
And the sky above,
And crystal streams below
Succumb—,
All will answer.
And what will you do?
Will you run?
Or man the gun?

It's the sun you want to feel—
Isn't it?

The Soil—Part 2

The Gift of Understanding

In my youth I hated *Papá*.
In my youth I hated the soil we lived
And worked on too.
In my youth I rejected the gifts *Papá* offered.
As a child I acted as a child—immaturely.
As often a petulant and emotional child will.

Petulance and emotion have since
Evolved into maturity and understanding.
As a man, I now embrace his gifts:
His love of the soil,
His need of hard work,
And I understand and forgive a hard man's way.

I have to remember to thank him
When I see him next,
When I return to the soil in which he lies.
And when he greets me, as I know he will,
I know what he will say:
Walk a little while with me, *M'ijo*,
Won't you?
And I will—gladly.
I will put my soft hand in his big, calloused one
And follow him,
And together we will once again
Walk the fields home.

THE SOIL—PART 2

The love/hate relationship I had with *Papá*
Was the same one I had with the soil.
I came from both.
At one time or another,
I've loved and hated both.

But as a man
With a son of my own,
I want to give him
My love of the soil,
My body's need of hard work,
And I hope he understands and forgives
A hard man's way.

In my youth I hated *Papá*.

In a Dream

The scarred, square table
Showed signs of
Having once been painted,
But that was long ago.
Only a few patches
Of faded blue
Remained.

It stood in the empty kitchen
Of the black, tar papered
Cabin we lived in
For a spell,
In my youth.

The cabin sat beside a road
Across from an asparagus
Field we worked
When the heat of early summer
Was not yet unbearable.

I was sitting at the table
As evening's warmth
And gathering darkness
Descended quietly on
My fractured dreams.

IN A DREAM

Within the soft, yellow glow
Of a naked, dangling
Incandescent bulb
I waited…

A cup of cold
Black coffee
Sat before me.

I was staring into
The spaces between
The echoes of my thoughts
And the shadows of a time
Too distant to recall,
Too close to forget.
They returned in dreams
To dissolve in the
Salty tears of sweat of
A migrant's laments.

I felt you
Before I saw you
Standing outside
The screen door,
Calmly watching me.

When I turned
To look,
You were there
As I remembered
As a child,
Thickly muscled,
Strong and vernal.

You asked
If you could come in
And I said no,
For I was
Angry with you—still.
It seems it's always been so,
But I don't remember why.

It seems I'm always angry
At something or someone;
God, people, life…
You'd think an old man
Would forget,

After all these years
Of memories,
Animosities, and regrets.
And what purpose
Do they serve?

And then you were gone
Into the ether
Of the darkness
And the warmth of
My dreams,
To wander where
Lost spirits roam.
When I turned away
And I woke,
Nothing remained
But my sadness
Laced regret.

But...*Papá*,
Give me another chance.
Return to me
In my dreams
Tonight, and this time
I will invite you in
To share my coffee.
And we will drink
Of the forgiveness
That's eluded us both.
And we will drink
To letting go of regret,
And the animosities
That eat us like
Battery acid in our guts.

IN A DREAM

Isn't that what you came seeking?
Isn't that why I dreamed of you?
I am free now.
I am free to
Love and embrace you
As you are to love
And embrace me.
Return from your wanderings
And know that I am here,
Waiting…

In a dream.

PARIS DREAM

Paris Dream

You found me working:
Cleaning up
Other people's messes.
It was a bathroom
To be sure,
And in the mirror
I looked and
Saw myself accursed.

What did you see, *Mamá*,
As you walked in the door?
Was it yourself in me,
Sixty years before?
The yoke of common labor
Once tight around your neck,
And then you found me
Worthy of little more,
The historical nature
Of what had come before.
You wanted so much more.

PARIS DREAM

And then you asked me
To go to Paris with you
And Dolores…
But hating travel
As I do
I said no.
And then wept
Bitterly for I knew
I was lost.

You found me working.

The Soil—Part 3

I Am New Life

My family worked the soil
On which I was born.
And under a waxing, corn moon
I was birthed, and within the soil
And the magic of the moonlight,
We were sustained.

When the autumn crispness
Made the grapes grow sweet
And the warm summer breeze
Gave way to winter cold,
I played in a migrant shack warmed by a coal-fed
Potbelly stove.
With backs bent, and sweat of brow
My older siblings worked ahead of me
In the cold fields until the sun disappeared
Beyond the coyote hills
That gave us shelter from the frigid winter winds.

When summer came, I entertained myself
In the dirt at the end of a row
Of sugar beets, asparagus
And a garden of vegetables and fruit.
I fed myself with infant fists of fertile dirt,

THE SOIL—PART 3

Chocolate mud ran down my chin.
Whether indoors or at the end of a row,
The soil always beckoned me,
Beguiled me.

The soil was enriched and nurtured by the blood
Of those who came before:
Four brothers and sisters who died
And were buried there.
And when they passed, their bodies
The soil consumed,
Feeding on their brown flesh,
Strong bones, and rich marrow.
While their deaths enriched the soil
And their spirits imbued within,
The soil lived with a hundred
Generations of our brown ancestors.
And the life once theirs
Became my own,
As I sat in the dirt at the end of the row.

Then, when I was old enough to hold a hoe,
I took my place beside my brothers and sisters
In the fields,
And we walked together through the rows,
A synchronicity of rising and falling hoes.

It was there, the cycle was complete.
The brown remains: ancestral spirits
And my sweat.

The brown remains: ancestral spirits
And my blood.
It was then the spirits of those
Who had come before—and mingled
And fused with my blood and sweat
And made us one and the same
Then again…new.
A hundred generations cumulative.
A hundred generations to rest.
A hundred generations
To form who I am today,
And tomorrow to be
Who I will become:
Somebody different…
To form someone new.

I am new life.

Saturdays

I get lost on weekends.
With no place I need to be:
Meetings, groups, or appointments.
I lie in bed, wandering aimlessly between
The stress of yesterday's schedule
And the serenity of last night's sleep.
With no place to go,
And still and day ahead.
It all swims in my head.

As light emanates from darkness,
And sleep dissipates into wakefulness,
The sun shining through the windows
Finds Timmy curled warmly at my feet.
I sense the other side of the bed
Is empty of its usual occupant.

I hear sounds coming from the kitchen,
Or are they coming from my dream?
Is it my dream you inhabit, my love?
And then come the scents
Of morning coffee from somewhere.
I listen closely and determine—yes.

It's tea for you
And coffee for me—cream and sugar.
It's Saturday morning, don't you see?

I roll over and dreams return
To find playful voices and poignant images
Of childhood.
I'm listening to muffled voices.
Momentarily, I can't place them.
The coffee scents mingle with the soft Spanish voices.
I'm in my childhood bed.
I can feel the summer morning sun
Splash softly on my face.

I'm running swiftly on a dusty, dirt road,
Chasing Salko, my boyhood dog.
I'm entering an immense, lush vegetable garden.
I'm eating watermelon with my brothers and sisters.
Enrique and I are climbing a haystack.
Mario and I are swimming in the cool, shallow
Irrigation ditch.

Linda and I are dancing in the dirt courtyard
To music coming from the radio on the porch.
Juan and I are tumbling down a hill
Behind our farm.

The laughter begins to fade
And the aroma of coffee once again
Invades my senses.
I hear the sugar spoon
Tinkling in a coffee cup.
I see *Mamá* and *Papá* at the kitchen table.
There's soft laughter.
I feel myself smiling.

SATURDAYS

Sweetheart, you're smiling.
Here's your coffee.
Can you smell it?
Sweetheart…?

It's tea for you
And coffee for me—cream and sugar.
It's Saturday morning, don't you see?

I get lost on weekends.

FRANCISCO'S SHADOWS

Francisco's Shadows

Although his steps are measured,
His hearing diminished,
And his legs weak,
He's undaunted,
He enjoys life…
Living with the enthusiasm
Of a child in a Sunday park
With a smile that can
Light up the neighborhood
On a sunny day.

Still, each morning he wakes at five,
Rain or shine.
He says it's late for him.
It was four, in his youth
When he was building houses,
But no need now.
No time clock to punch.
Not that he's retired…
Not completely anyway.
He still builds…
Kitchen cabinets here,
A bathroom there.
Nothing big, just enough
To pay for the vices that remain.

FRANCISCO'S SHADOWS

Just enough to feel vital,
To feel alive.
He doesn't want life
To pass him by.

He sleeps well.
He retires early,
And darkness passes
Unaccounted for.
Winter winds are spent—now quiet,
And the bitter cold has given way
To softer steps
And warmer days.
It's morning now.
He walks into the kitchen,
Fills his coffee mug and
Carries it to the porch
Where he stands for a moment,
Observing the darkness,
Engulfed in the emotions
He's always had.
They well up suddenly,
In his throat…
Choking his air,
And what they're all about
Is a mystery he will never understand.
Maybe it's from childhood,
A harsh *Papá* he never
Got along with.

He's always wondered
But understands some things
Need no return address.

So he breathes deeply
And sniffs the air,
Like he's often seen…
The coyotes that roam the park
In the early morning
Or late at night.

He closes his eyes
And smiles.
All around are the familiar scents
Of pine and oak sap,
And the fresh smells
Carried on the waves of
A revitalizing breeze
Coming unimpeded from the west.

He knows the rebirth
He feels is spring making its way
Back from its travels in the east.
He eases into his favorite chair
And waits…
A patient man,
Having less to do
With what is left.
And what is left,
He guards for
What he hopes…

FRANCISCO'S SHADOWS

A thousand tomorrows.
It's still dark
But won't be for long.
He loves to watch the
Sun come up…
It takes him back to
A time he thinks he can still recall:
A harder time—on a small, brown dirt farm
Far away from this porch,
In miles and time.
It might have been a love story
He read or watched
Late one night
When he couldn't sleep.
He isn't sure anymore.
How time and space
And the blowing wind
Have had their way with his past:
Something he thought
Or someone he knew:
Something he lovingly held
In his hard, callused hands
And tender heart,
For a short while.
It might have been longer,
But everything is short
When viewed from
Fading memories,
Yesterday's regrets,
From a time gone by.

And yet, he must let go
For he knows today's desires
Hold tomorrow's promises.

The slight breeze is cool
Against his flannel pajamas,
Warm against his deeply bronzed skin.
He inhales and welcomes
The spring air
And blows it cool across
The cup,
And he can feel the warmth
And strong scent of coffee
As it wafts back into his nose
And face.
Another of his latent joys…
The scent and taste of
Steaming black coffee
On a cool morning.

He sips and watches,
Sips and dreams,
Until the darkness gives way
To dark shades of gray,
And almost imperceptibly
As if by sleight,
Images begin to appear,
But he isn't sure
If ancient optics are to blame,

FRANCISCO'S SHADOWS

Are imaginary or real.
And so he breathes
Ever so deliberately…delicately
So as to not disturb
The magic unfolding before him.

A robin comes to rest
On the deck railing.
It sits and watches him for a long moment
Cocking its head right, then left
Before flying off to find its breakfast.
A blue jay squawks urgently,
Hiding somewhere high in the distant pines.
Across the way is the park
And now he can just begin
To see the outline of
Budding blackjack oaks,
Oklahoma redbuds, and Bradford pear trees,
Masquerading as malevolent shadows.

The developing image of a doe appears.
The only movement
Is the flick of a feathery tail
And slight bending of her
Long slender ears,
Front, then back,
As she listens to the sounds
Around her.
They watch each other
Pretending each is not there.

And then a gray squirrel
Scampers across the wet,
Decaying leaves
And disappears up an oak trunk.

And now the dark shades
Turn to lighter grays
As the sun begins to illuminate
The thawing landscape,
Waking from frozen sleep.

Like a rose opening up
To the warming sun,
He is watching a new day begin.
And although he has seen
More of them than he can remember,
It's vital to him, he be there
When each new one begins,
For he is searching
For secrets that evaded Solomon,
And he suspects ride the breeze
Or might be discovered in the shadows
That dissipate with the morning light.
With his cup lifted to the heavens,
He reverently makes the sign of the cross,
Brings it down,
Peers into the remaining darkness,
And takes one last sip.

Coffee finished,
New life stirs within him
And spring is hope for another season.

Although his steps are measured,
His hearing diminished,
And legs are weak,
He's undaunted.
He enjoys life…
Living with the enthusiasm
Of a child in a Sunday park
With a smile that can
Light up the neighborhood
On a sunny day.

It's About Respect

He Says, Manuel

It's all about respect,
He's often heard saying,
Now that they're gone
And don't call
Or come around.
Now that I'm secluded
It's hard for me
Not to be included.

They could drop a note,
Talk about the family,
Share a picture of
Places that they've been.
Send me greetings
And tell me how they're feeling.

They could give a call—
Hear my voice,
And maybe ask how I've been…
Growing old, you know,
And how is the weather?
Oh, it's been cold and
I can't stay warm.
Everything is deliberate,
Everything is planned.

IT'S ABOUT RESPECT

I don't know why
But nothing seems spontaneous anymore.
And these creaky bones give me pain,
But why complain?
Some I know have it worse.
Really, I'm doing fine.
And how about you?
Send me a sign.

It would be nice to hear your voice,
Or touch your letter—see your words.
They all mean so much
To one who has so little.
Most I had is all but gone,
But health is good.
I won't complain.

I walk the dog every day
And stay busy around the house.
You remember me.
If I'm not building or fixing something,
I feel the worse,
Like I'm no use,
And the smelly trash
Is put out on Tuesday morning,
To the curb and the day is done.

IT'S ABOUT RESPECT

The young have lost their
Understanding of us, I fear—
Those of us who carry a belly load of hard time,
And time is like a heavy weight
That stoops our shoulders.
Mine once were strong and straight
And carried you around the house,
But now I sit by the kitchen window
And watch the rain,
Or sit among strangers in the
Corner coffee house
Down the street.
I read the paper and watch
Them and the traffic moving past,
And I wonder if
They're watching me.
The strangers and the traffic,
We are all just moving past…

And yes, it's time I fear,
Now that I have only
One good year…and it is slow
And often stops.
Now that I have more
Time behind that ahead.
And now my time is in reflection,
And an old man's affliction.

IT'S ABOUT RESPECT

The young fear nothing
And life is all about them
And what they do,
And where they go:
Busy schedules,
Raising families.
It's all for show.
The young have no understanding
Of those who came before:
Walked on creaky floors
And through these old
Wooden doors:
Went to work
And paid the bills
So they could have a life
And a better place.
It's no disgrace.

It's about honor too,
The kind you give to elders
Who deserve…and sometimes don't,
When they have little to give
In return: bones brittle,
Hands that shake,
And a walk that is hunched,
And somewhat tilted,
Like a lilting boat,
Lost to the currents of the sea.

It's about respect earned…and sometimes not,
But respect given nonetheless.
It's our Mexican family way.
And if I honored you in
Youth, will you
Honor me in my waning years,
When my dreams of youth
Have disappeared?

It's not about whether I was
A good or great man.
I know I wasn't.
And yes, I did try
But being flawed,
I wasn't always right.
You may not think,
Because I talk so loud,
I don't understand,
But believe me, I do.
For like ocean currents
That crash on rocky shores,
They first retreat,
But soon return for more.
To you, I implore,
It's about forgiveness
Now that I want yours,
And maybe you need mine.

For all my faults,
I'm still the only father
You will ever have.
And of you, my child,
I'll have no more,
So I don't want to let you go.

I know I've not always been kind:
The sensitive man you
May have wanted
As a child,
Or even now,
Mature in years.
Yes, I know I've often
Said too much
And been too critical,
Spoke too soon
Without thinking
Of your feelings.
Yes, I know I learned it from
Papá, a hard man too.
And today, I struggle to be worthy
As he probably did
When he saw his destiny
In the comfortable sleep that
Came so easily...
And he must have known
Would take him soon.

Ashes to ashes,
Dust to dust.
If not reborn,
All is rust.

And yes, it's time I fear,
Now that I have only
One good year…and it is slow
And often stops.
Now that I have more
Time behind that ahead.
And now my time is in reflection,
And an old man's collection.

In spite of his heavy hand,
I accepted and loved him desperately
For I've always seen our destinies
Interlaced and intertwined.
I came from him
And in the end,
Will return to him
And together we will
Walk the fertile lands of
Our Outlook farm,
A heaven we once knew.

IT'S ABOUT RESPECT

And one more thing,
Let's tell the truth.
As I came from him,
You came from me.
As I am him,
You are me.
And when I looked into
His cloudy, foggy eyes
And saw the fading light
Flicker ever so slightly,
I saw myself recumbent
And needing you,
As he needed me.

Come see me, I'd like to say.
And let's sit down and talk
About the old days
And how much I loved you
And how much I hope
You still love me.
In the end, what do we keep?
All we have
Is what we give
And what we give,
Who can take?

IT'S ABOUT RESPECT

Respect, honor, and love.
In the end, what more is
There to trade?
And let me admit,
I will take nothing with me
When I depart
To the time ahead.

To a time beyond,
But I wish to leave
For you…my family,
Something behind;
My respect, love, and honor.

It's all about respect,
He's often heard saying.

The Search for Absolution

Uneasy—you lie there, poised on Adirondack chair,
Awkward heap of loosely gathered, gaunt and
Spotted skin,
Stretched over misaligned and broken bones—
A farmer' life, your fare.

Frail and withered—little the man you used to be.
Jaundiced, sunken eyes staring across the room—
At what?
Haughty arrogance—hard man once,
Still unwilling to see or to believe.

Do you remember me?
Child of your loins,
Child of Thanksgiving's pleasure—long past.

Hello and smile, I place my hand on yours:
Bony, limp, arthritic—as it is.
I gently squeeze and hold it firm,
Asking once again for you to confirm.

You raise your head in deaf response
And look my way,
Serpent tongue slowly runs across dry lips
Stretched over gums where teeth once were.
A faint smile you disguise, but why?
What do you hide?
What do you fear?

A wanting child of youth, were you too deprived
Of what I ask and seek?
To easily give…Was it not given?
You blink beady eyes to feign response.

"Are you my child"
I watch them ask (So insolent!)
You, white child of one so dark,
Of my loin or *Mamá*'s indiscretion?
It shall remain unknown to me
And is long forgotten by her.

And ask of me…
Having less within than what you ask,
Little as it may be—
Less than you foresee.
Deceit, remorse, and shame.

What runs through senile mind:
With pursed lips, and reluctant smile,
Searching back, memory to unlock?
Do you permit the luxury of soul's searching…
Of one forgiven?

It was long ago (my youth) I do admit.
But those hurt, especially young, see and remember…
Memories more tender.
(Memories forever etched in a secret, midnight vault,
Sparked by ancient triggers.)

THE SEARCH FOR ABSOLUTION

Your steely glare, your leather belt:
The price I paid for spilled milk
Or broken windowpane.
What do you feel?
Who do you see
When you examine me?
A young, defenseless boy,
Doing what young boys do.

Did you think ill done in dark finds no mark
(Or not remembered?)
Or believe all is swept away with cool night breeze
As it draws through summer's open windows,
Blowing gently
Across your sheet-draped, muscled body
As you brazenly lie,
Naked and asleep, sins dissipating, imperceptibly,
As light creeps upon the dark.

Do stooped shoulders and bent back release you
From the brutishness that was your part?
Has deafness, muffled child's cries, and echoed
Nightmares that torment sleep?
No matter, they return…
They ride bitter winds that blow cold from me.

Are you spent as you labor with each breath?
No more hate to fuel your cruelty?
I ask,
Not for cause,
Not for show,
Just to know.

In humble silence you preserve your Ancient
Dignity.

Uneasy—you lie there, poised on an
Adirondack chair.

To the West

When I looked out toward the west,
Darkness clouded my eyes
And my soul was troubled.

Long I stood,
And alone,
On the river bank.

Like a snake—the river,
Crooked and twisted,
Drenched in orange sun
As it descended
Behind a farm house,
Barn, and tall fields of corn.
As it disappeared…
It carried the weariness
Of my life's labor with it.

My soul descended with the sun.
My heart disappeared into the flowing river.
And then I heard a voice ask,

"When the night comes,
Where will you lie?
When day dawns,
What will become of you?"

TO THE WEST

I saw nothing in the horizon
For me—a brown child of the dirt.

When I looked out toward the west,
Darkness clouded my eyes
And my soul was troubled.

Afraid Again

I woke up afraid again, *Mamá*.
It wasn't the wind I'd been hearing,
But my cries in the deep of dark
Of a lonely hillside I'd been wandering:
Looking for my home.

It wasn't the rain
That wet my cheeks,
But tears that flooded the desert
Of my confidence.

And *Mamá*,
I'm not a child anymore.
I'm a man with my own,
But I still wonder how to face a day
I know I'll never own.

I woke up afraid again, *Mamá*.

Special Thanks

A special thanks to Jill Twist and Jill Flores for their invaluable help putting this book together.

About the Author

Ramón Mesa Ledesma was born in Toppenish, Washington, into a family of fifteen brothers and sisters. His formative years were spent in labor camps throughout the Pacific Northwest. He served in the US Air Force as a crew chief on a KC-135A Tanker/Refueler. During the Vietnam War, he was stationed at Fairchild Air Force Base, outside of Spokane, Washington. He flew out of bases in Thailand, Okinawa, and Guam. He attended Spokane Falls Community College in Spokane, Washington, and Eastern Washington State College in Cheney, Washington. His undergraduate studies were in history, sociology, and anthropology. His graduate studies were in counseling.

Ramón lives with his wife, Kendra, a high school mathematics teacher, and two dogs and a cat on ten acres in rural Sedro-Woolley, Washington. He is retired from his counseling practice and now spends his time writing, interviewing his siblings, and rummaging through their shared past, in search of more stories to tell.

www.ingramcontent.com/pod-product-compliance
Lightning Source LLC
Chambersburg PA
CBHW021141130626
46554CB00005B/1604